Breakthrough Time

BREAKTHROUGH TIME

UNLEASHING THE VALUE OF BUSINESS OPPORTUNITIES

A Teamwork Sharks® Business Novel

Michael Goodfriend

Copyright © 2016, Michael Goodfriend, All Rights Reserved

ISBN-13: 9781537612492
ISBN-10: 1537612492
Library of Congress Control Number: 2016915203
CreateSpace Independent Publishing Platform
North Charleston, South Carolina

Table of Contents

Prologue – Time to Go ix

Chapter 1   A Beautiful February Day 1
Chapter 2   Unexpected Visitors 4
Chapter 3   Decision Time 8
Chapter 4   Now or Never 11
Chapter 5   Houston, We Have a Problem 13
Chapter 6   We Made It 15
Chapter 7   Like Father, Like Son 19
Chapter 8   Houseguests 22
Chapter 9   Universal Space Travel 27
Chapter 10 It's About Time 33
Chapter 11 The Business of Time 37
Chapter 12 The Teamwork Sharks Process 40
Chapter 13 Mining for Business Opportunities 44
Chapter 14 Family Time 49
Chapter 15 The Nominations Are In 53
Chapter 16 Will We Get There In Time? 55

Chapter 17 A Great Idea · 58
Chapter 18 And The Nominees Are… · · · · · · · · · · · · · · · 64
Chapter 19 Opening the Can of Worms · · · · · · · · · · · · 68
Chapter 20 Dinnertime · 70
Chapter 21 Batter Up · 73
Chapter 22 The Reason We Are Here · · · · · · · · · · · · · · 77
Chapter 23 The Might to Reunite · · · · · · · · · · · · · · · · · 79
Chapter 24 Missing Pam · 87
Chapter 25 And the Finalists Are… · · · · · · · · · · · · · · · · 89
Chapter 26 Empathizing with God · · · · · · · · · · · · · · · 94
Chapter 27 All Work and No Play · · · · · · · · · · · · · · · · · 97
Chapter 28 Stepping in the Bucket · · · · · · · · · · · · · · · 99
Chapter 29 The Kickoff · 103
Chapter 30 Time Guides · 106
Chapter 31 Making Cryogenics Obsolete · · · · · · · · · · · 108
Chapter 32 Generational Family Reunions · · · · · · · · · · 111
Chapter 33 Space Travel Acceleration · · · · · · · · · · · · · · 115
Chapter 34 A Working Lunch · · · · · · · · · · · · · · · · · · · 119
Chapter 35 Executive Session · 121
Chapter 36 Time for the Sharks to Circle · · · · · · · · · · · 125
Chapter 37 And The Winner Is… · · · · · · · · · · · · · · · · · 130
Chapter 38 Wrapping Things Up · · · · · · · · · · · · · · · · · 135
Chapter 39 Some Time with Gary · · · · · · · · · · · · · · · · · 137
Chapter 40 A Party That I Will Definitely Forget · · · · · 138
Chapter 41 Next Steps · 141
Chapter 42 Change in Plans · 144
Chapter 43 Just Another Day · 147

Epilogue – All Is Right with the World · · · · 149
Appendix · 151
Acknowledgements · · · · · · · · · · · · · · · · · · · 169
About the Author · · · · · · · · · · · · · · · · · · · 173

Prologue – Time to Go

Karena gave her husband a look that made him wonder if she was going to leave him forever.

"Gary, I know you don't want me to go, but I need to see him."

Being married to Karena had its challenges, but Gary knew it was in her nature to be adventurous and stubborn.

"Okay, Karena, but I might not be here when you get back…."

CHAPTER 1

A Beautiful February Day

Mid-February in Houston, Texas is like paradise compared to the oppressively hot summers. It was a sunny day with temperatures in the high 60s. Little did I know that the day's feeling of paradise would soon fade.

I heard Kay's voice as she politely barged into my office suite. "I need some coffee but none of that flavored stuff." Kay Breeden and I each had our own consulting businesses but began working together about two years earlier, partnering on the Teamwork Sharks®.

My cell phone rang. "Hi, honey," I said, greeting my wife on the phone. "I'm just about to start a meeting with Kay." Then I said to Kay, "Pam says hi." Back to the phone, I said, "Honey, can I call you back? Okay, love you."

Kay said, "Tell your lovely wife hello for me, and that we all need to get together again."

"We'd love that," I said.

"So, what's on the agenda for today?" Kay asked.

"We need to discuss the plan for our next Teamwork Sharks assignment."

Kay and I model what great teamwork is all about. We have a common belief that certain business opportunities and results can be achieved only by working well together as a team. We disagree a lot, but that always leads to something better than where we started. Our personalities are quite different, which means we complement each other as much as we frustrate each other.

The Teamwork Sharks, patterned after the television show *Shark Tank*, is a process during which leaders present a business opportunity that can *only* be achieved by working well as a team. The process helps leaders mine and uncover cross-functional business opportunities to accelerate improvement in business results. Participants within an organization compete against each other to articulate the most compelling case for a business opportunity at the Teamwork Sharks event. Kay and I, the Teamwork Sharks, select a winner—the business opportunity that we believe is the best, biggest, and most probable to drive better business results.

The concept of the Teamwork Sharks started two years prior when I wrote a *Goodfriend Insights* newsletter article titled "Could Your Leadership Team Survive the Shark Tank?" I was scheduled to make a presentation on teamwork to a CEO roundtable, and the leader of that roundtable, Sal Mira, read the article and asked if I could lead a Teamwork Sharks event with his group instead of a more typical presentation. My wife had recently introduced Kay Breeden to me, and this seemed like a perfect opportunity to see how we would work together.

Remembering our first Teamwork Sharks assignment was like going back in time. But that was in the past now. Kay was in my office to discuss our next Teamwork Sharks client, ABC Custom Piping. ABC makes piping out of round steel bars by manufacturing a hole through the middle of the bar, a process called trepanning. They also perform other machining operations to the bar. These pipes are used for drilling in the oil and gas industry.

As we walked into the small conference room to start our planning meeting, Kay said, "Tell me more about ABC Piping."

"ABC is a $250 million company," I said. "Barry Young is the president and owner. They have three machining shops, and each specializes in a different type of machining. Barry has asked us to conduct a Teamwork Sharks Leadership Challenge. He wants to invest in his next generation of leaders so that his assistant shop managers, planning specialists, controllers, and other management team leaders can become more influential as the company pursues rapid growth."

"Sounds like an ambitious goal," said Kay, "and one that we can help him with."

I uttered the fateful words, "We can knock out our plan in an hour or two and be home for lunch."

If only I could have gone back in time to change those words, but as the expression goes, the best laid plans of mice and men often go awry.

CHAPTER 2

UNEXPECTED VISITORS

WE WERE WORKING THROUGH THE timeline of activities for ABC when the door to my office suite opened. I heard a couple of unfamiliar voices, so I got up and poked my head out of the conference room and saw that the voices belonged to a man and a woman, maybe in their early fifties, a little younger than me.

"Hello," I greeted them. "Can I help you?"

The man said, "Are you Mike Goodfriend?"

He sounded a bit nervous. I am not exactly the type that makes people nervous. I have always seen myself as a regular guy who is no better than anyone else.

"Yes I am," I said.

His voice trembled as he spoke, and he could barely get the words out. "I . . . I can't believe I am meeting you in person . . . in the flesh. This is unbelievable."

Is this some stalker from one of my presentations or something? My fears quickly subsided when I realized that he looked and sounded familiar.

"How can I help you?" I reached out to shake his hand and put him at ease.

"This is my sister, Karena. My name is Marcus...Marcus Goodfriend." He paused. "We are your grandchildren."

I laughed at the absurdity of such a claim. "Is there a hidden camera here? Who put you up to this? I have only one son. Sam is nineteen, and I am quite sure he doesn't have a couple of kids I don't know about that are old enough to be his parents' age."

Kay overheard the conversation and didn't want to miss the opportunity to see what this was about. I looked at her with a grin, and said to the two visitors in a very sarcastic tone, "Unless you came back in time from the future...."

Marcus and Karena looked at each other then said in unison, "We did." Taking the lead, Karena said, "How did you guess?"

I was thinking this must be a practical joke. "Can I see it—what you traveled in? Is there a hot tub time machine like in the movie?" Then, in a more serious tone, I said, "Kay and I have some work to do. Not sure who you are and why you are here, but we really don't have time for this. Thanks for stopping by." I couldn't suppress my sarcasm by that point.

Karena looked me in the eye for what seemed like an eternity then rushed over to me, crying, and gave me a big hug. "I never got to meet you, and my dad always speaks about you. I know you don't believe that we are your grandkids, but we're so excited to see you for the first time!"

Marcus jumped in. "Grandpa, we can't be here for very long. We came back in time to see you in 2016 because we need you to help us. Actually, we need both of you. Our company is on the verge of doing something special, and we need the Teamwork Sharks if we are going to make this happen. Will you help us? Will you both come with us to 2085?"

Kay looked at me, her eyebrows raised, and I think she must have sent me a telekinetic video message of her twirling her finger around her ear in the universal motion that says, "They're crazy."

I wasn't quite ready to dismiss these two. There was something about Marcus and Karena that made me want to be patient for a few moments to see how this played out.

"Okay," I said, "why don't you show me your driver's license or some other form of ID, if you really are Marcus and Karena Goodfriend." Karena looked a little puzzled and then remembered from history class in college. "They did away with driver's licenses and physical ID cards in 2020 because it became so easy to create fake IDs and passports. Everyone has a chip implanted in one wrist, at birth, embedded with a unique identifier. Police, immigration, department stores—everyone uses these chip readers to identify people." She paused to let that settle in. "And my maiden name is Goodfriend. I am married to Gary Rosen, and I have grandchildren myself."

Now I was intrigued. "So, if you are my grandchildren, tell me something that only you would know about me."

Karena continued, "Dad told us that when he was a baby, he was in one of those baby carriers that snapped into a car seat base, or you could snap it out to carry it around. He said he was sleeping on a car ride, and when you came home, you brought the carrier into the house and set it on the living room floor. You picked it up when it was time for you to go to bed, but it tipped over, and he landed on his head. He told us that you told him he had an indentation in his forehead for a little while. He also said you joked about it when he got older, saying things like, 'Imagine how smart you would have been if I hadn't dropped you on your head.'"

I instinctively laughed at this memory. "I loved telling that story, but when I saw that dent in his forehead, I thought I had injured him for life." When I caught myself reminiscing about this story, doubts flooded in. "Karena, as far as I know, you may have met Sam yesterday, and he told you that story."

I glanced at Marcus and was struck by his look of determination. That look instantly reminded me of Sam playing baseball, being in the on-deck circle ready to face an unhittable pitcher.

Marcus jumped in. "If I just met him yesterday, would I know that my dad has a mole on the bottom of each of his feet, that Sandy Koufax was your favorite baseball player when you were a kid? Would I know that you met Grandma at Toastmasters?"

"You do know things that very few people would know," I said, "but you're not expecting me to believe that you are my grandchildren, are you?"

CHAPTER 3

DECISION TIME

———

Marcus knew time was running out. "Grandpa, since I am almost your age, I hope it's okay if I call you Mike. Let me cut to the chase since we have to be back in an hour to the location we call the Timeport. My dad started a company in 2052 called Universal Space Travel. We call it UST for short. He is eighty-eight now—I mean, in 2085, he's eighty-eight. Karena is the CEO, and I am the Chief Technology Officer. Karena and I each bought a forty percent share in the company from Dad. Dad owns the remaining twenty percent."

Kay, trying not to think about whether time travel was even possible, was interested to hear more about UST. "So why do you need the Teamwork Sharks in 2085?"

Karena responded, "Because UST owns the rights to Timeport, a scientific technology for time travel. Dad bought the rights from a childhood genius friend of his named Josh. You probably know him, right?"

She glanced my way, and I nodded, thinking about Josh and Sam when they were four years old constantly laughing as they created new ways to use "poop" in a sentence—not exactly a picture of Josh developing a ground-breaking design for time travel technology.

"We need to commercialize this technology now," Marcus added, "because we only have about five years before the competition develops time travel technology solutions. We want a five-year head start."

"But why do you need us?" I asked. "Surely you have better resources in 2085."

Kay interjected. "Let me guess. You want as many ideas as possible. You want to commercialize one offering in a big way, and you want it to scale up quickly. You know you can do that if you work well as a team cross-functionally. You need the Teamwork Sharks to increase the commercialization options and help you select what to commercialize, right?"

Karena and Marcus smiled and had hopeful looks on their faces.

Being the natural skeptic that I am, I knew it would be irrational and illogical to believe Marcus and Karena. But my gut was telling me to think twice about it.

Kay, on the other hand, had a look of adventure on her face. "We should call our families to tell them we are going to see them in the future!"

I took out my phone to call Pam and Sam. That's when Karena chimed in. "There's no need for that. You will return right back to this time when you come back from 2085. You won't be aware of the passage of time. It will seem as if you've never been gone."

Marcus was eager to bring us into the future. "We better get to Timeport right now or we will miss our transit window."

Karena agreed. "Yes, we better get going. My husband told me that if I'm late and don't return until 2095, he won't be there when I get back. Are you ready?"

CHAPTER 4

Now or Never

I WAS STILL THINKING THIS might be a joke. "Do we have to go to NASA or something?" Marcus explained that Timeport was a distortion in the space-time continuum uniquely engineered for this trip.

"Just think of it as if we dug a tunnel between 2085 and now," Karena added as we left my office building. "After the tunnel has been open for six hours, the walls begin to lose their integrity. That will start happening in about fifteen minutes."

I chuckled and shook my head. "You actually had me believing you for a while, but it's rush hour in Houston, Texas. We can't drive anywhere to get to any Timeport in fifteen minutes."

Karena smiled. "We knew we were coming to see you at your office, so we uniquely engineered a Timeport tunnel to open right here behind the trash dumpster in your building parking lot."

Marcus added, "When we activate the Timeport, we will only have a short time to walk through the opening before it automatically secures. When the Timeport is open, it looks like a bright light. Once we walk through the opening, we will be in 2085, and we will be in the Timeport Operations Center at UST in Arizona, what we call the TOC. So it's pretty much now or never. Are you ready to go?"

I looked at Kay, and she looked at me and nodded. It felt like we were about to jump off a cliff and hope for the best. I looked at Marcus and Karena. "This better not be a hoax for a hidden camera TV show…."

We walked to the back of the office property behind the garbage dumpster, and a bright light appeared. Marcus said he would walk through first to tell those operating the TOC that the rest were on their way. But just as Marcus was about to walk through, the light began to fade. He looked worried. "Hold on, everybody. The light is not supposed to do that."

CHAPTER 5

Houston, We Have a Problem

When Sam Goodfriend founded UST, he needed a young, bright aerospace engineer. That was Roberto Rodriguez. Little did Sam know that Roberto would still be at UST thirty-three years later as the Vice President of Galactic Strategy.

Roberto, who served as acting CEO while Karena traveled to 2016, nervously paced the floor hoping that all was going well. Marcus and Karena knew this was a risky venture. If this failed, the consequences for UST would be disastrous, not to mention a complete waste of all that investment and time.

Roberto walked into the TOC to find Carolyn, the TOC manager, gazing at a screen with a look of impending doom on her face.

Glancing up at Roberto, she said, "Karena and Marcus may be in danger. Timeport is malfunctioning. The astrointegrity readings indicate that the timehole is losing its integrity. The Timeport window will only be open for another fifteen minutes, but it may not be safe for them to return."

Marcus was the timehole engineering expert for UST. Roberto was originally an aerospace engineer, and timehole science did not exist when he went to school, but once an engineer, always an engineer. Roberto had been learning as much as he could from Marcus about the Timeport technology. So, in addition to being acting CEO, his knowledge of Timeport made him a great backup to Marcus in case he was hit by a skycar—or didn't return from a time travel trip.

Roberto, always calm, quickly instructed Carolyn to adjust the romino levels in Timeport to reduce the disproportion in the astrointegrity levels. Carolyn did as instructed. They waited. Finally, she breathed a sigh of relief. "It's working."

In 2016, Marcus saw that an adjustment had been made, and he felt confident we could go forward. The four of us walked through the timehole into the TOC. The first thing I saw was the lettering on the wall: "The Eva Goodfriend Timeport Operations Center."

CHAPTER 6

WE MADE IT

NOT WASTING A SINGLE MINUTE, Karena contacted Gary using something called a holocom, a holographic communication device. Gary appeared as a holographic image. Karena announced, "Honey I'm home."

Gary sounded relieved, but never losing an opportunity to joke, he said, "Oh good. I didn't think you were coming back to 2085. I guess that means I'll have to end my relationship with the beautiful blonde weather girl on TV."

Karena, who was quite used to his sarcastic humor, responded, "Too bad for her. You would be such a catch for her."

Gary shifted the conversation as if he was communicating with a fellow secret agent. "So, did you kidnap the 'packages'?"

"Yes, Gary, my grandfather and Kay Breeden are here in the room with us, and they have been given top secret clearance to know who you are."

I jumped in. "Gary, I hope I get a chance to meet you and your family. I am not sure what the protocol is about time travel and all that, but I hope I get to spend time with Karena and you, as well as Marcus and his wife, and all your kids and grandkids."

Karena needed to get us to the briefing meeting, but she needed Gary to do something for her. "Go get Dad and bring him here to the office," she said. "Tell him his father wants to see him."

As we walked down the hall with Karena, Kay said quietly to me, "This day is way more interesting than I thought it would be."

"That would be an understatement," I replied.

Karena showed us into the conference room. Marcus was there to greet us along with the leadership team members who introduced themselves one by one: Roberto Rodriguez, the Vice President of Galactic Strategy; Shannon Block, the Chief Marketing Officer; Rory Williams, the Chief Operations Officer; Dianne Ferrini, the Chief Financial Officer; Martina Bryan, the Vice President of Technology; and Rashad Ford, the Vice President of Sales.

"Let's get started," Karena began. "First, I want to say thanks to all of you. We did it. Timeport is finally here. Now we have to take advantage of this opportunity. We have struggled with how we should make Timeport a viable, profitable line of business for UST, but the time is now. We know our competitors are working on time travel technology, but we are probably five years ahead of them. That may seem like a lot of time, but not when we have no options ready to take to market for Timeport. Mike and Kay, thank you for being here."

Karena paused to choke back a few tears. "You have no idea what it means to me that you are both here. Not only because we need the Teamwork Sharks more than ever but because I am getting to work with my grandfather."

She then composed herself. "This has been an emotional day for all of us. My dad is coming to the office now so he can see his father for the first time in many years. Then, if it's okay with Kay and Mike, we would like to invite them to stay at our house so they can rest up. Roberto, tomorrow is still Thursday, right?"

Roberto nodded and joked, "It looks like the Timeport didn't fry that part of your brain!" Everyone chuckled, and he directed his next comments to Kay and me. "Tomorrow, we'll get started and fill you in about Timeport. The good news is we don't need you to sign a confidentiality agreement because you won't remember any of this when you return to 2016."

I finally had an opportunity to get a word in. "Thanks, Karena, Marcus, Roberto—thanks to all of you gathered here. You can only imagine the number of questions we have right now. But this part about not remembering any of this when we return to 2016—I'm not sure I like that. I want to remember this for the rest of my life!"

"I know what you mean, Mike," said Karena. "I will never forget this day either. For now, we need your help, and we know you can't help us unless we answer your questions.

When will you and Kay be able to discuss your plan for the Teamwork Sharks to help us commercialize the Timeport technology?"

I looked at Kay and said "Friday?" and she nodded her head. "Friday it is," I said.

CHAPTER 7

Like Father, Like Son

As we all walked out of the Milky Way Conference Room, Marcus asked Karena if they could meet in her office privately. They went ahead of us down the corridor, and Roberto acted as a tour guide for Kay and me. "On your right is our Timeport research lab. Karena and Marcus will be showing you this tomorrow afternoon. Over here on the left is the command center for our core business. I will tell you more about it tomorrow. Straight ahead is Karena's office. Mike, you can wait in there for Sam to arrive. Kay, why don't you and I explore whether a 2085 cup of coffee is any better than in your time?"

When I walked into Karena's office, she asked me to take a seat next to Marcus, and told me that Sam was about five minutes away.

"I can't wait to see him," I said, "but I am also uneasy about seeing my nineteen-year-old son as an eighty-eight-year-old."

Marcus looked me in the eye. "Sam is still your son, even in 2085. We know this may be a little odd for you, but keep in mind that you probably talked to Sam yesterday in your time, but he hasn't seen you since…." Marcus caught himself. "Let's just say this may be a more emotional reunion for him than it is for you," he added.

A young woman came into Karena's office very excited. "Excuse me for interrupting. Oh, hi, Mr. Goodfriend, I am Mayra, Karena's assistant. Karena, Sam and Gary are in the parking lot."

Karena thanked her and said, "Go find them and bring them here directly. No interruptions from anyone now—no exceptions."

After Mayra left, I said, "I am sure your father told you how close we have always been … uh, I mean … we were. We played baseball, played video games, talked politics."

Just then, two men walked in. We all stood up. I don't think I even saw Gary. Sam and I looked at each other for a surreal moment.

Sam broke the silence. "Dad!" I immediately went to Sam, and we gave each other a big hug.

"Dad, this was always my dream when I bought the Timeport technology from Josh—to see you again after you died." Sam started getting emotional, and there was not a dry eye in the house.

It was shocking enough to hear myself referred to as having died, but I wasn't prepared for what I heard next.

"Marcus and Karena have wanted to meet you for a long time," said Sam. "Mom told them all about you before…."

Marcus interrupted. "We were lucky to spend a lot of years with Grandma before she died."

Karena said, "I know you have lots of questions. It's eleven a.m. My thought was that we all go to my house and make it a family day. Dad will stay over. Then, in the morning, we will get to work. Think of this as a business trip where you get to spend some time with family as well."

Tired of waiting for an introduction, Gary said, "Mike, I am Gary Rosen, your grandson-in-law. I would be happy to take you and Kay to the house now. Karena, Marcus, and Dad will be there soon."

CHAPTER 8

HOUSEGUESTS

"Welcome to our home!" Gary said as Kay and I walked in.

Karena and Gary had a beautiful house in a city called Space City, Arizona. Gary shared with us that Space City was in the desert in the middle of nowhere until space transportation businesses began to relocate there because of the dry climate and access to engineering talent. Although Houston had been Sam's home for many years, he believed that if UST was going to be viable, it needed to be where his customers were.

Technology advancements were apparent in the home of 2085. Intelligent robots were part of the household. These robots looked and acted more like the C3PO character in the *Star Wars* movies of my time.

"Gary, what do these robots do?" I asked.

"They do household chores—cooking, cleaning, mowing the grass—whatever needs doing. Watch me. Rob, take out the kitchen garbage to the outside garbage can and put a new garbage bag in the kitchen can." Rob the robot responded, "Yes, Gary." He executed the task to completion.

Gary showed me some of the other technological changes in the preceding twenty years that made life easier and more convenient. He demonstrated how to communicate to anyone in the house by clicking on your watch that connected the microphone and speakers in each room to your home network.

When Rob the robot returned from his task, Gary instructed him to clean the pool.

Gary was quite a host. "We'll print you a change of clothes on our 3D printer. Let's see what you want. He walked up to a 60-inch screen and said "Target." He gave voice commands to get to the catalog for clothes where a holographic, three-dimensional model demonstrated how the clothes looked and fit. He purchased the clothes by scanning the chip implanted in his wrist, then, using voice commands, he said, "Print on 3D Max." After making a few adjustments to the printer, the clothes printed within five minutes. Kay and I stood there holding our clothes, speechless at the ease with which all this was done.

"Let me show to your rooms now so you can change," said Gary, smiling at our wonderment. "Karena and Dad are on their way."

Karena and Sam walked in. It was very strange to see my son as an elderly man. My mind just couldn't comprehend this. I had so many questions, and I couldn't contain my curiosity.

"Can I start asking questions now?" I asked, full of eagerness.

Sam took the lead. "Marcus and his wife Debra will be here momentarily. Maybe we should wait for them. By the way, it will probably make you happy to know that the Astros finally did win a World Series. You and I went to Game 7 together when they clinched it—one of the best sporting events of my life. I wish we had time for you to go to the moon to play some baseball there on this trip."

I was excited. "You can play baseball on the moon?"

Back in 2016, I played baseball in the recreational Houston Hardball League. The most recent team, the Angels, had won seven championships in the last eleven seasons. Even at fifty-seven, I still loved playing the game, and I still wanted to win every game.

We were all talking baseball when Marcus and Debra walked in. I think I started my first question before they had a chance to close the front door. "Sam, when I came through Timeport and arrived in the TOC, I saw that it was named after an Eva Goodfriend. Who is Eva?"

Sam replied, "The TOC was named after my wife Eva. I wish you could have met her."

I asked, "So she's no longer with us?" That was a strange question for me to ask since I was no longer with "us" either.

Sam smiled, got a little teary-eyed, and seemed to struggle for words when Marcus stepped in for him. "Our mother passed away five years ago. We miss her every day. We were just as lucky to have her as a mom as Dad was to have Grandma as a mom."

"Eva was perfect for me," Sam said, his voice wistful. "We had so much in common—family, friends, sports, travel. She was everything I wasn't, and vice versa."

Although Sam had aged quite a bit in sixty-nine years, he seemed the same. He was still very easygoing, always smiling, and seemed to find the positive in everyone he met.

We had a delicious dinner prepared by the kitchen robots, and my questions continued. I asked about all their kids and grandkids, and if I was going to meet them. I wanted to know how my grandkids had met their spouses.

I had never seen Kay so quiet. As surreal as it was for me, it must have been like being in a movie for her. After a while, she seemed perfectly comfortable with my family, and she jumped in. She wanted to know how people shopped, how they did their banking, and when the driverless skycars replaced the automobile. Sam, Karena, Gary, Marcus, and Debra were very patient and answered each of our questions.

Karena then said, "It's getting late, and we all have a big day tomorrow."

"Yes, there has been enough excitement for one day." I responded. "Sam, I'm dying to know if your cousin George served his whole fifteen-year prison term, or did he get out on parole?"

Kay looked excited. "Wow! Even the Goodfriend family has a bad apple."

"Who is Cousin George?" Sam asked. "Dad, are you feeling okay?"

"Just checking," I replied. "I just wanted to make sure this isn't a dream."

CHAPTER 9

Universal Space Travel

When Kay and I rode in Karena's skycar the next morning on our way to UST, I thought about how lucky we were to have this experience of being in 2085.

Karena then interrupted the silence. "Even though we are family, I want you and Kay to know we need you as any client would. We calculated what your typical fee in 2016 dollars would be today, and it would be $4 million."

Kay liked that idea. "Count me in for a couple of mil."

Karena spoiled Kay's potential windfall. "Sorry, Kay, but we can't run the risk of you taking money back to 2016. That could change your future and our present. But we do need your help. Timeport is a transformative technology, and we believe this will be an experience of a lifetime."

I looked at Kay to get her reaction, but Karena continued. "Mike, my father told us that it was because of you that he started UST. He said watching *Star Wars* movies with you sparked his interest in the possibilities of space travel. We are now at the cusp of transforming the human experience through time travel technology. This can be our legacy. Please—I need you and Kay to help us."

Before I had a chance to say anything, Kay made her commitment. "Mike, you can count on me. Let's do this."

It was 7:50 a.m., and Karena assured us we would be in great hands. Roberto was waiting for us at the door. "Welcome to your first consulting day at UST. How about some more of our 2085 coffee?"

"I guess," Kay replied, somewhat unenthusiastically. "With all the disruptive technology advancements in seventy years, you'd think someone would have invented great-tasting coffee by now!"

Roberto took us to his office. We settled into a pair of upholstered chairs pulled up to his desk, and Roberto told us how lucky he was to have worked at UST since he graduated college in 2052. He also felt honored to work for my son. "Sam is one of a kind," he said. "During my job interview, Sam told me he had made a lot of money on Wall Street, and he had recently founded UST to provide services to the growing number of private spacecraft owners traveling to the moon and beyond. Sam shared his core purpose, which hasn't changed." He looked up at a plaque on the wall and read it aloud: "Making your mission as effortless as it is weightless."

Roberto described the core services that UST provided its customers:

- Mission planning
- Astronaut services
- In-flight meals, communication, and entertainment
- Spaceport accommodations and excursions
- Spacecraft storage, fueling, and maintenance

Roberto explained, "As one of the first employees here, Sam wanted me to understand that one of our core values was teamwork. He said that playing baseball really shaped his view about the importance of individuals working together as a team to achieve one goal. He shared a story about one of his Little League teams called the Florida Gators. He said the team won the championship not because they had the best players but because they had the best teamwork."

Looking at me, Roberto said, "Sam was a disciple of your teachings about teamwork." Roberto pointed to my teamwork model, TeamScene®, posted on the wall:

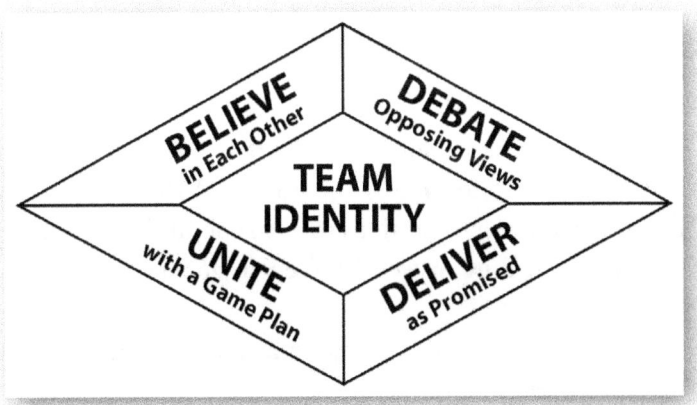

Roberto continued, "We still use your model today. We are organized by core service teams—a mission planning team, an astronaut services team, and so on. The model provides these teams with a common approach for working together effectively as a team."

"Thanks for sharing that," I said. "It's humbling to know that my teamwork model is still in use today, so many years later. In fact, here we are a lifetime later, and all that you've described is recognizable to me. I'm humbled and thrilled at the same time."

"I am very glad you're here—both of you," Roberto added with a smile. "We have not made enough progress with our goal of increasing customer wallet share. Too many of our customers buy only one of our services. For example, they buy mission planning but not spaceport accommodations, or they buy astronaut services but not mission planning. We want each of our customers to buy all of the services they need from us and not from our competitors. Our service lines are not collaborating well enough as a team to capture a greater amount of wallet share from our customers. How can we accomplish this goal?"

"Great question, Roberto," Kay responded. "We should make some time to discuss this further. In the meantime, I've thought of some questions you can consider in relation to your business. Your answers will help us guide you:

- ▶ Do your metrics currently measure customer wallet share?

- If so, is it clear who is accountable for increasing customer wallet share?
- Have you considered the pros and cons of reorganizing your business structure to increase market share?"

Looking at me, Kay said, "Mike, can you think of any others?"

I consulted my notes. "I do have two more questions, Roberto. These have to do with processes and technology.

- Have you considered the cross-functional and end-to-end process improvements necessary to serve customers effectively through multiple service lines?
- Is your technology in alignment with working cross-functionally to increase wallet share?"

Roberto responded, "Let me do some thinking about this before we talk again. I audio recorded our conversation." He tapped his watch and added, "It's all right here." He couldn't help remarking, "I see you've taken notes on paper. Not sure where you found a pen and paper in 2085, but I am guessing Gary Rosen had something to do with that! Old habits die hard for Gary."

No wonder we hit it off with Gary, I mused with a smile.

Rory arrived for our tour of the facility. We stood and thanked Roberto for his time.

On our tour, we met the specialists in each of the service lines, including mission planners, spacecraft specialists, inflight specialists, and accommodations specialists.

Karena joined us along with Shannon Block, the Chief Marketing Officer, who spent about forty-five minutes explaining each market, its potential, UST's market share, the market's spaceport, and the buying patterns of customers in that market. We were quite interested in the Alien Origination market. These customers were no longer Earth residents. As permanent residents of the moon and Mars, they traveled to Earth for business and pleasure.

Because our questions may have continued for hours on that subject, Karena thought it best to interrupt so that Kay and I could break for lunch.

CHAPTER 10

It's About Time

After lunch, we met with Marcus and Karena. Comfortably full, and trying not to feel drowsy, I said, "It's good to see that a hamburger in 2085 is just as good as it was in my time."

Kay bristled at that. "Why did you say *was* as good and not *is* as good? That time still exists, and we are going back to it, right Marcus?"

"Yes, you will be going back," Marcus replied. "But we need you to stay for now to help us with Timeport. The year 2016 will be there waiting for you when you go back. You'll return to the exact spot where you were when you came through the tunnel to 2085."

"The other tenants are going to wonder if I live behind that dumpster in the parking lot," I joked to ease Kay's anxiety.

Marcus was eager to tell us about Timeport. He was like a kid with a new tech toy. "Timehole science has only been around for twenty years now. I was so fascinated by the science of timeholes and the possibilities they presented that I went back to school about ten years ago to take a few courses just to satisfy my curiosity. I liked it so much I decided to get another degree in timehole science. During class, I daydreamed about engineering a mechanism to open and close the timehole in a systematic way so that people could travel back and forth in time. I also thought about how well that would fit with our existing business in serving private spacecraft owners."

"I believe you knew Sam's childhood friend Josh," Marcus continued. "Dad told me that Josh had always been a creative thinker, but he did not have a science background. About five years ago, Josh and I were talking one day about timehole science. He was curious about it and asked several questions. A week later, he came back with a fully developed engineering design for something called Timeport—the technology needed to travel back and forth in time. Since Josh was a digital engineer, his design did have some flaws, but ninety-five percent of it was flawless. More importantly, it was an engineering breakthrough for time travel."

"I still remember when Josh, who was eighty-three at the time, showed me the design and explained it to me. He said that he had developed several designs in his day, but he had never been more sure than he was of the design for Timeport. The design creates temporal tunnels using vortal acceleration around gravitational waves."

Kay interrupted. "I'm an engineer, but I have no idea what any of that means. You might as well be speaking an alien language!"

I looked at Kay and said, "Thanks for saying what I was thinking. I feel better now. I thought I was at some science convention where I was the only one who was confused." I was about to make a joke about engineers and slide rules but stopped myself before I lost all credibility with my audience.

Marcus continued. "Let me explain it another way. Think of it as a tunnel between time periods that supercharges the speed at which a person goes to the other end of the tunnel before it begins to break down. Timehole integrity breakdowns were the impediment to time travel. That's why Josh's design really was an engineering breakthrough. As soon as I saw the design, I thought about the different ways we could commercialize this technology.

"But when I presented it to Dad, he immediately thought of seeing you, Mike, and Pam and Eva. Dad was a strategic thinker, even at eighty-three. 'Marcus,' he said, 'I am going to make Josh an offer for Timeport. This could make the $28 billion cryogenics industry obsolete—overnight. No one will need to freeze him or herself for the future if they can travel back and forth in time. If we get to market first with this technology, and we do it safely, we can capture most of that market.'"

Marcus wasn't finished. "Dad thought he made Josh an offer he couldn't refuse. Strangely, Josh rejected it and made a counteroffer for half of Dad's offer and a commitment to keep his identity secret as the creator of the design. Josh didn't want to be hounded by every scientist interested in timeholes and gravitational waves. The only people who know that

Josh invented Timeport are Dad, Karena, me, and the two of you. Everyone else believes that Dad acquired the technology from an unknown scientist who wanted to keep his identity private."

"Oh, great," Kay said sarcastically. "Now I am going to have nightmares of spies torturing me to pry that information out of me."

CHAPTER 11

THE BUSINESS OF TIME

Karena took over. "Marcus became our Timeport technology leader, and my focus has been to get us ready to tackle the commercial challenges. In the last five years, our focus on Timeport has been on developing and testing the technology based on Josh's design. This has not been easy because we have had to acquire equipment while not tipping off manufacturers or suppliers that we were building a vortal accelerator. We also tested this technology at each step to ensure it was safe, and then, before a human test, we used a robot to make the trip back and forward in time. We conducted three human tests of going back in time before coming to see the two of you, but we had never brought anyone back with us from their time to ours. You two are the first. You're time-traveling pioneers who are making history as we speak."

"Your first three test subjects must have been brave souls," I observed.

"They were," said Karena. "Three of our executives volunteered. What better way to set an example than being willing to take a risk for a business opportunity with a lot of potential."

Karena continued. "As far as we know, Timeport is the only time travel technology that is ready for commercialization. We believe we have the advantage in this race, but until we generate revenue from Timeport, we are in the same position as everyone else. We need to identify Timeport business opportunities and develop strategic plans for capturing the market for those opportunities. That is why we need the Teamwork Sharks."

"But why do you need us?" I asked, glancing at Kay, who nodded her agreement that she'd been wondering the same thing. "Sam already knew about the Teamwork Sharks concept, and could guide you through it. Besides, there must be other strategic thinkers in 2085. What makes us necessary?"

Karena was very confident in her response. "The two of you are the pioneers of the Teamwork Sharks, and we are the pioneers of time travel. We need your instincts in seeing the Timeport business opportunities through a pioneering lens. That's why we need both of you."

I looked at Kay and said to Karena, "You've convinced us again. What's the next step?"

"Timeport can be a solution to many of life's problems and opportunities—so many that it is a challenge for us to focus. We must offer solutions that protect life in the present, past, and future. We have no focus and no priority.

We want a Teamwork Sharks process that involves all of our executives, directors, and middle managers. We want a plan from the two of you by tomorrow morning so we can get started right away. Be ready to present it to the Executive Team at nine a.m."

CHAPTER 12

THE TEAMWORK SHARKS PROCESS

———

THE NEXT MORNING, KAY AND I arrived at UST with Karena and went directly to the Milky Way Conference room for our meeting with the executive team. When we walked in, we were surprised to find all the executives waiting for us, even though we were forty-five minutes early.

I looked at my watch to make sure the time travel hadn't caused it to malfunction. Confirming that it showed 8:15, I asked, "Did the meeting time change from nine a.m. to eight?"

Roberto immediately responded as if he were speaking for the group. "We are all pretty excited, so we thought we'd get here early so we could start as soon you get your coffee."

Kay nudged my shoulder. "See, you're not losing it yet, Mike," she quipped. Kay seemed to already have a relationship with Connie, the automated coffee machine in the conference room. "Connie, give me two large black coffees… and none of that flavored stuff." After Connie provided the coffee, Kay sipped it and said, "This is a bit better than yesterday's brew. Not bad."

"Thank you, Kay," Connie responded.

I took a sip of mine, and we took our seats.

I began the meeting with some history. "This all started back in 2014. There was a popular television show called *Shark Tank* where entrepreneurs made presentations to five angel investors to get startup or additional capital to grow their businesses. These investors were tough negotiators. They were very blunt when they didn't like a business idea. It was up to the entrepreneurs to convince one or more Sharks that their business could grow rapidly and profitably with an investment of capital in return for a share of the company. The Sharks weren't interested in an idea that the entrepreneur had dreamed up on the way to work. They wanted verifiable details—sales history, profit percentage, intellectual property protections—that sort of thing. In other words, they expected the entrepreneurs to present a viable business plan backed up by real data.

"With my focus on teamwork, I saw a need for this type of process to help organizations take advantage of business opportunities, but with a twist: opportunities that could be achieved only by working well as a team.

These business opportunities could be externally focused like adding a new line of business or entering a new geographic market. The business opportunities could be internally focused like improving business processes or restructuring roles and responsibilities to reduce costs.

Kay and I observed in our business consulting experiences that the best opportunities were cross-functional but were often not being realized because of resistance to change, focus on everyday execution rather than long term strategy and not having an effective approach to making compelling business cases that overcome bureaucratic obstacles.

"Kay and I were a great team from the beginning. Our first Teamwork Sharks session was with a CEO roundtable. There was one winner, and he told the group after the session, 'The discussion today was like one of our roundtable sessions on steroids.' We quickly began providing this service to corporations to address two common challenges."

Luckily, they still had whiteboards in 2085. I wrote two of our Teamwork Sharks solutions so that everyone could see them at the same time:

- The Teamwork Sharks Leadership Challenge
- The Teamwork Sharks Strategy Challenge

I explained the first bullet point: "The **Teamwork Sharks Leadership Challenge** is a six-month program for clients that want to invest in their next generation of leaders. The program involves one-on-one coaching, group skill building, and a competition for leaders to demonstrate what they had learned by making a case for a business opportunity that could only be achieved by working well as a team. This also had to be a team that they would lead."

Pointing to the second bullet point, I said, "The **Teamwork Sharks Strategy Challenge** is a process to carve out the client's unique recipe for strategic differentiation, a Teamwork Sharks event to identify the best, biggest, and most probable business opportunities and initiatives, and then a must-win focus on execution."

As soon as I put down the marker, and before Kay had an opportunity to present the process for the first phase of the Teamwork Sharks, the questions started coming.

Shannon asked, "What does the agenda look like?"

Roberto asked, "My staff have some great ideas. Can they be involved in this?"

Rory had a question also. "Will we be getting some education about time travel science and our technology before we present any ideas?"

Marcus asked, "Do we present this to our people in teams or individually?"

"Those are all great questions," I said, "and I think you'll see that many of them will be answered when Kay presents the Teamwork Sharks process."

Kay started by saying, "I want to thank you all for welcoming us into your time and into your company. You have been very gracious. Karena and Marcus, thank you for making me feel welcome in your family."

Karena responded, "Kay, we are glad you feel welcome in our family and in our business. Now might be a time for a short break. Let's reconvene in ten minutes."

CHAPTER 13

Mining for Business Opportunities

The executives actually made it back on time, so Kay was prompt in starting the meeting. "The Teamwork Sharks process will make a difference for the growth and profits of UST, but more importantly, Mike and I can help UST change the fabric of your customers' lives by making time travel available to an increasing number of people. Time will no longer be in a straight-line sequence.

"Timeport will be a goldmine within UST. In this Nominations of Business Opportunities phase, you are looking for people at UST to propose business opportunities for Timeport. We believe there will be much enthusiasm among your people to explore and mine for business opportunities. This should be encouraged and enabled, since the more opportunities proposed, the better. Their ideas might spring from their experience at UST or from a personal experience that has shaped their personal lives.

"So as the Teamwork Sharks, Mike and I want any individual or group in the company to nominate their business opportunity for Timeport, in writing. The nomination does not need to be a detailed business plan, but it does need to persuade us through a compelling business case that includes both quantitative and qualitative measures."

Kay glanced around the table to make sure everyone was still with her. "Here are our thoughts on what will make a compelling business case in a Teamwork Sharks nomination."

She wrote the following points on the whiteboard:

Describe the business opportunity:
- The need it will serve
- The market it will play in
- What it will offer
- The marketplace advantage for Timeport and UST by being the first to market for time travel

Explain why you are compelled to lead this:
- Tell your story for this business opportunity
- Why it matters to you
- Why you want to lead it

Align your message to make this a win for your key stakeholders:
- The Teamwork Sharks
- The executives
- Likely Timeport customers
- The business units/functions at UST

Why this can ONLY be achieved as a team:
- how cross-functional the teamwork will need to be
- the roles of the team members

Estimate the ROI (return on investment):
- projected investment
- revenue and cost models for the business opportunity

Kay explained the rest of the Teamwork Sharks process. When she finished, there was silence. You could almost hear a collective gulp from the executives, not because of what the process involved but because it was hitting home of how significant Timeport was in terms of the opportunity, potential, and challenge.

When Kay took her seat, I said to the group, "I know this is a lot to think about right now, but I'm sure you're already brainstorming how to put this process in place. Does anyone have any thoughts about the criteria we should use to evaluate the nominations?"

Dianne Ferrini, the CFO, responded first. "How about cash flow and profit?"

Marcus added, "We can't alter history when we travel back in time, because that could affect today."

Roberto offered, "We also can't leave anything from our time in the past. I guess we could call that no environmental time garbage."

Rashad Ford, the VP of Sales, suggested, "Safety for all should be a given, but I think that should be one of the criteria if we are going to grow this business quickly and securely."

Then it was Karena's turn. "If at all possible, I believe we should make a positive impact on society. This is a real opportunity to do that."

Kay walked to the whiteboard. "So, it sounds like these are your success criteria." She wrote the following on the whiteboard:

- Cash flow and profit
- Do not alter history when we travel back in time
- Safety for all, both past and present
- No environmental time garbage
- Positive impact on society

Kay turned to the group. "Are there any others, or are these good?"

After some silence, Karena said, "I think those cover everything."

Shannon said, "I'm good with the criteria, but I have a question. Did I understand you correctly when you said that anyone can submit a nomination for a proposed strategy, including our direct reports, a customer service representative, or a spacecraft technician, for example?"

Kay nodded. "You should involve as many people as possible from the executives to the front-line staff." She glanced around to address everyone at the table. "You never know who might have the best idea, and no one is an expert on the strategy for a time-travel business. And don't forget, the winner receives the Teamwork Sharks Tooth Award. I am guessing we can produce that on your 3-D printer!" Her eyes lit up in a smile.

Marcus followed up by asking, "What is the deadline for nominations?"

"One week from today," I replied, "at noon. Let your teams know."

Shannon Block blurted out, "It's breakthrough time!"

Karena just looked at her and said in a droll tone, "Yes, Shannon, it is time for us to breakthrough."

Shannon laughed. "What I meant to say is that we should have a theme about this when we ask for nominations. Let's call it *Breakthrough Time*." The executives smiled and nodded. Some of them had already gotten it because they were familiar with the creative way that Shannon's marketing brain worked.

"So it sounds like there is a theme," I said. "Martina, I am guessing that, as the VP of Technology, you might be able to get Kay and me a communication device so that anyone at UST can contact us."

CHAPTER 14

Family Time

Kay and I were exhausted by the end of the day. We had an endless stream of people coming by to ask questions about the Teamwork Sharks process and to share their ideas. We also met with Roberto to discuss his thoughts on the customer wallet-share questions we posed to him the previous day.

Gary picked me up to go back to the house. Roberto had offered to show Kay around and buy her dinner while I met more of my family members. As Gary and I were flying back to the house in his skycar, I began to yawn from the long day. Gary laughed and said, "Better get a power nap now while you can, Mike. No rest for the weary. Sam is coming over tonight—our kids and grandkids too. It's your turn to answer questions, and they have lots of them. Our kids know who you are, but the grandkids don't. They are too young to comprehend time travel, much less a man who is about the same age as their grandparents but is the grandfather of their grandmother. Heck, it's pretty confusing to me. So you'll just be our friend Mike to our grandkids."

We could hear the noise of small children as we walked in the door. Sam greeted me at the door and gave me a hug before he said to me, "So did you keep up the average work today?" Sam was referring to the managing partner of the CPA firm where I worked after graduating college. He used to walk the halls in the office and bark at anyone who walked by. I can remember it like it was yesterday, "Goodfriend, keep up the average work." Although we knew he was joking, you always wondered if that day he might be serious.

Karena introduced us to their kids. "This is Mike, your great grandfather. Mike, this is our son and our oldest child Louis and his wife Natalie, our middle child Ana and her husband William, and our youngest child Clara and her husband Porter." Each one came up to hug me. They gave me a real hug, not just an obligatory hug.

Louis then said, "A lot of people don't get to meet their great grandfather, but those that do surely don't meet him when he's 126 years old but looks like a fifty-seven-year-old."

Ana then chimed in. "This is a first, though. We are the first to meet their great grandparents through time travel."

Clara then added, "Yeah, this must be how the astronauts felt who were the first to land on Mars."

I responded to all of them, "Then maybe you can imagine what it's like for me feeling like I am on an alien planet with all of you that I have never seen before, yet you all instantly feel like family. And in my time, 2016, we have so far only put a man on the moon, and that was w-a-y back in 1969 when none of you were even thought of yet. It's remarkable to hear you talk about the first astronaut to land on Mars!"

Gary then announced that dinner was ready. As I walked into the dining room with Sam, I said, "Ana and Clara? That's not a coincidence, is it?"

Sam shook his head. Ana Clara was an exchange student from Brazil who lived in our home when Sam was about ten years old. She had been like a big sister to him. Sam then said, "Ana came to visit my family and me when Karena and Marcus were young kids. They used to call her Aunt Ana."

They had set up two tables in their big dining room, one for the adults, and one for my great, great grandchildren. Karena walked me over to the kids' table. Karena introduced me to each of them as her friend Mike. "This is Marty, who is Louis and Natalie's only child. Marty is six years old. These are Ana and William's children. Jack is four, and Ida is two. These are Clara and Porter's children. Sarah is five, and Abraham is three." Ida was the name of my grandmother.

This was a surreal experience. I was here in a future time that I could not really grasp. My son was almost seventy years older than when I last saw him. I was with family and all of my descendants that I could never imagine having.

None of us had any idea what was going to happen with the business opportunities being proposed, but Timeport had already changed my life and my family's in a way that we never would have dreamed possible.

While enjoying my second helping of apple pie, I felt a tug at my shirtsleeve. It was four-year-old Jack, who wanted to tell me something. "Mommy told me that my great, great grandfather's name was Mike. He played baseball until he was an old, old man. I'm going to be a baseball player too so I can be just like him." It made me think of Pam, and all those years of playing in the Houston Hardball League. I wish I could tell her, "You see, it was all worth it now, wasn't it?"

CHAPTER 15

THE NOMINATIONS ARE IN

IT HAD BEEN AN EXCITING week working with the team at UST. After the executives met with their teams to discuss the Teamwork Sharks, Kay and I distributed the nominations template so that all the employees could begin formulating their ideas. Kay and I conducted brainstorming discussions with about forty-five people to glean their ideas about business opportunities for Timeport.

At this stage, our purpose was to encourage brainstorming, provide innovation methods, and coach the UST employees on what we look for in evaluating submitted nominations.

As the deadline approached, Kay and I knew there would be quite a few nominations submitted. We were not disappointed. At 10:00 a.m., the nominations began to pour in, thirty-two in all.

Kay and I split up the nominations, and for the next eight hours, we read them and made notes. During that time, one of us would pause our silent reading for a moment and say things like, "Wow," or "Life in 2085 will never be the same," or "I can't believe I am here for this," or "What an idea!"

We had lunch brought in, and we worked throughout the afternoon. Right around 6:00 p.m., I yawned and looked at Kay. "Ready to call it a day?"

She nodded. "Yes, I'm feeling a bit brain-dead right now, but it's hard to stop because there are so many good ideas here. That idea titled Bring Your Pet Back to Life – In the Future could be a real winner."

"Yes, but the relationship fixer opportunity could be a big hit too," I added.

Kay admitted that tomorrow would be a tough day since we could only select nine nominees for interviews.

I added, "To help us make our decision, let's keep in mind that we have to distinguish between ideas that have great emotional appeal and those with quantum growth potential. It won't be easy."

We had just gathered our things to depart for the day when Karena barged into the conference room. She seemed very anxious and distraught. "We have to leave right now. It's Sam…."

CHAPTER 16

WILL WE GET THERE IN TIME?

My mind raced as we got into Karena's skycar to go to Marcus's house where Sam had been visiting his grandchildren. Karena's comline in the skycar beeped. It was Marcus. "Sam is in bad shape. Get here as soon as you can before it's too late."

"We're on our way," said Karena. "We'll be there in ten minutes."

Those ten minutes took forever, and I didn't say a word the entire time. It was one thing for me to come to the future and see my nineteen-year-old son as a wise and successful grown man. It would be another thing to face the death of my son.

I reminisced about Sam's birthday party when he was four years old, staged like the Olympics. I thought of when I was manager of his champion Little League team when Sam was the starting pitcher in that game. I remembered being so proud of my teenage son as a counselor at Camp Impact, a day camp for kids in broken or abusive homes, and for being president of his youth group. There was also his decision to attend college at Louisiana State University. Most of all, it was great to see that he had become everything a father would want in his son. He had a beautiful family and was successful in business. More than that, his business was about to change the world.

When we arrived at Marcus's house, the three of us jumped out of the car and ran to the door. Marcus was waiting, and he opened the door for us as we approached. We followed him to the guest room.

Marcus told me to brace myself before I opened the door. Feeling like time was running out, I burst into the room to see my son. I almost passed out with shock when everyone yelled, "Surprise!" It took about five seconds for my mind to realize that Sam and my entire 2085 family were throwing me a surprise party. The feeling of fear throughout my whole body was quickly replaced with exhilaration when I realized that Sam was not dying.

My happiness turned into faux anger at all of them. "I could have had a heart attack and died!"

Sam laughed and said, "So what. Remember, you're technically already dead." Everyone joined in the laughter.

Not to be outdone, I kept it going with some sarcasm of my own. "Yeah, but if I die of a heart attack in 2085, I won't be able to return to 2016."

Karena stopped laughing and had a look of real fear on her face. She looked at Marcus as that same look of fear overtook him. She and Marcus immediately left the room to huddle.

Five minutes later, they re-entered the room and motioned for Sam, Kay, and me to go into the other room. "Mike is right," she said the moment she closed the door. "We thought the risk would be much lower to our present reality by minimizing our time in the past. That is still true, but if someone we bring from our past to our present dies while in our time, then we can't return them to their present which could permanently alter their future—and our present."

Marcus jumped in. "Wait a minute. Everyone settle down. I have an idea. Karena, I will meet with Roberto tomorrow, and we will have a risk mitigation strategy for you by the end of the day. Mike and Kay, don't let this slow your efforts in any way. Now let's go enjoy your party. We're probably scaring the others with our secret discussion, and we don't want to do that. Welcome to 2085. We are glad you and Kay are here."

CHAPTER 17

A GREAT IDEA

"The party's over," Kay said when we arrived at UST the next morning. "Time to get back to work."

I was on a high and a low that morning. My family had given us a great party, but I'd had a bit too much to drink, and I was definitely feeling hung over.

But that's what coffee was for, and today, for some reason, it didn't taste so bad. Connie the coffeemaker had upped her game, her artificial intelligence getting smarter as it adapted to our requests.

Kay was eager to present her first recommendation for interview. "Mike, this is a great business opportunity that can only be achieved by working as a team, and the opportunity is exponential. The idea is called Time Guides. It will change people's relationship with history. I could hardly enjoy myself last night at the party because I was so excited about this."

Kay described the idea submitted by Ray Wong, the Director of Mission Planning. Ray had a bachelor's degree in History from Arizona State. He proposed the idea that time-travel tourist guides, called Time Guides, would take tourists back in time to witness famous events, such as the first Super Bowl, the day Sandy Koufax pitched a perfect game in baseball, the Lincoln and Douglas debates, Martin Luther King's "I Have a Dream" speech, the crucifixion of Jesus, and the coronation of Queen Elizabeth I of England in 1559. Like a good salesperson, Ray made sure to present examples that Kay and I had knowledge of as opposed to those that happened after 2016.

In selecting nominees to interview, we were looking for ideas that presented a compelling business case. That had to start with defining the need for the business opportunity. The need could be a problem that the idea would solve.

But that was not the case here. In this case, the need was an opportunity to allow people to experience historical events through the technology of Timeport. The Time Guide would only take one or two people at a time to the destination, and the tour could not be more than six hours. As we learned when Karena and Marcus came to get us in 2016, the Timeport tunnel begins to break down after six hours.

Ray had done some research on the number of people pre-paying for private space travel in the early twenty-first century, and based on that data, he estimated that fifty to 100 people a year would buy a trip. Ray's plan also set an expectation for five new destinations a year for four years before we re-assessed our strategy and plan going forward.

Kay then continued, "If you are excited now, wait until I explain the economics. We have always expected Teamwork

Sharks nominees to make a compelling case on the cost versus benefit. Well, each time-travel guided trip would have a fee of $400 million for one person and $600 million for two people. That is a lot of money even in 2085. To determine the price, they used a benchmark of what the first private citizen paid in 2006 to travel to the international space station. Anousheh Ansari paid $20 million in 2006 for that opportunity."

Kay sweetened the pot for this idea. "Because very few people could actually experience this, Ray had quite a brainchild. After all paying customers have visited a specific destination, a film crew would return to film the event in 3D so that it could be watched using virtual reality technology. UST would make the video available at $1,000 per view, or the equivalent of fifty dollars in our time. Ray anticipates at least fifty million views per year for each destination. Five new destinations would be added each year for four years, so that's twenty archived destinations by the fourth year."

Kay went to the whiteboard, and in vintage 1980s style, she wrote the calculations without using a calculator. The average revenue breakdown for the first year would be as follows:

$500 million per trip x 75 trips per year x 5 destinations = $188 Billion
$1,000 per video view x 50 million views x 5 destinations = $250 Billion
Total Revenue in Year 1 = $438 Billion

I had to stop her. "Kay, even as a former accountant, those numbers are making my head spin. What is all of this in 2016 dollars?"

Kay tried to make it simple. "One dollar in 2016 is worth twenty dollars in 2085. The core business model in 2016 dollars would generate about $100 million in annual revenue, whereas the Time Guide business would generate $22 billion in 2016 dollars in year one, an increase of 22,000 percent. The numbers are mind-boggling, and sound quite achievable, but we will need to gain a better understanding of these calculations during the interview."

Kay explained why she was so excited about this opportunity if it was achievable. "Since the revenue would double every year for years two, three, and four, the total revenue for the four years would be a little over $6 trillion, not bad for a company that in its core business at ten percent growth would generate a little over $9 billion. That's almost a 72,000% increase over a period of four years."

"I see where you're going with this," I mused. "Did Mr. Wong outline the cost basis for this venture?"

"He did, but I do have some questions." Kay returned to the table to shuffle through her notes. "He outlined that only one tour guide would be needed for each destination since there would be only fifty to one hundred days per year of time travel for each destination. He also recommended two additional tour guides who are cross-trained in multiple destinations for vacations, family emergencies, and the like. That's only seven tour guides needed for a business that will earn $438 billion."

"What would be the other functions assigned to each destination?" I asked.

Kay looked at the nomination notes. "A security officer will go on the trip to act as a bodyguard and to ensure the traveler returns. A historian will research the destination event in minute detail to know the weather, the Timeport opening location at the destination, the exact date and time of the event, and other pertinent details. A travel agent will map out step-by-step instructions for the tour guide based on the historian's research, and a wardrobe specialist will ensure that the wardrobe of the tourist matches what was worn at the time of the event. We wouldn't want a woman to go to the crucifixion of Jesus in a mini skirt, for example, or anywhere before the Sixties, for that matter!"

"Is that the whole team for the destination?" I asked.

"No, they will also need a Timeport engineer who ensures that every technical detail is taken care of. This person will work with the Timeport Operations Center to ensure the reliability of the time tunnel to the destination. Ray also discussed the need for a non-dedicated finance representative to ensure that payment, liability waivers, and insurance are all handled in a timely manner. He also described the need for a mechanical quality auditor to audit the reliability and integrity of the Timeport as well as a Time Guide Process Quality Auditor to ensure that all the other roles described above are doing their jobs. What do you think his cost forecast is for the estimated number of trips in the revenue projection?"

Kay looked at me, a smile tugging at the corners of her mouth. "You'll never guess," she said, not waiting for a reply. "It's only $4 billion compared to $438 billion of revenue. That's a ninety-nine percent profit margin."

Kay could barely contain her excitement for this nomination. But there were a few questions we needed answers to, which we would glean during the interview, such as the cost of life insurance (customers would likely need to be self-insured), how to prevent an "escape" by a customer to live in a destination time, and how to screen customers to ensure their integrity.

"So, Kay, an effective case for the Teamwork Sharks is a business opportunity that can be achieved only by working well as a team. I am guessing that Ray made the case that each of those roles needs to coordinate with each other, and the criticality of sharing every bit of information across all departments—the travel agent with the security officer, the historian with the wardrobe specialist, and so on. Has Ray made provisions for that?"

"You got it," said Kay. "So this one makes the cut for the list of nine to be interviewed, right?"

I got quiet for what seemed like an eternity to Kay. She told me later that she wondered whether I was seriously considering rejecting this one, and if I did, she would consider me crazy. When I saw her eyes get big with incredulity, I said with a chuckle, "Just kidding. Of course we will interview Ray. Like we're not going to consider a really good opportunity for UST to make $438 billion in the first year Timeport is open for business!"

CHAPTER 18

AND THE NOMINEES ARE...

IT WAS MY TURN TO make a recommendation. The next business opportunity was important for any society—solving crimes.

Kay settled in her chair to listen, and I launched in. "The business opportunity was proposed by Gabri Willis, the manager over Spaceport Accommodations and Excursions. When she was a young girl, her father was murdered. Here is how she described that horrific event. 'I was in the house at the time of the murder. My father told my mother and me to go hide in the attic. We heard it all, but neither of us saw the murderer. The police were never able to charge anyone with the crime.'

"Gabri is proposing that UST work with the FBI and local police departments to identify the high priority cases that have reached a stage where solving them is unlikely. UST would employ an elite team of detectives who would plan and investigate the trip to the past to observe the crime and film it in progress without being observed. UST would take a law enforcement officer as a witness and a subject matter expert. The police departments would pay UST a project fee for the services provided. A price per project was not submitted in the nomination, and there was no assessment of the market for this service. Gabri did propose that the fee cover the costs to UST for the salaries for the security team members and the use of Timeport."

"We'll need more details," Kay commented.

"We will," I said, and continued. "Gabri has a lot of passion for this proposal, and it clearly has an opportunity to make a difference for society and the families affected by crime, but it's a little short on data."

"It sounds like you have some reservations about this one," said Kay. "Get to the point, Mike. Are you recommending this one for interview, or do you think we should reject it?"

"I am recommending against interviewing Gabri even though it is a very noble idea. She didn't really build a convincing business case. I have some concerns. It sure seems like solving the crime would alter history and therefore impact the world of 2085 and beyond."

Kay agreed. "I'm with you on this one. Will you be giving her feedback when we communicate who we're going to interview? Just let her know how we came to our conclusions and what she can do the next time UST is considering business opportunities for Timeport."

I agreed. "Our role as Teamwork Sharks at this phase is to be impartial judges, not to take ownership over great business ideas that are not fully baked. That is the primary lesson that organizations have to learn—that great ideas have no real value unless a compelling business case can be made to advance the idea. That's what leadership development programs and innovation coaches should focus on."

Kay and I continued this process for another four days. As planned, out of the thirty-two nominations, we found nine viable business ideas whose originators we would interview. Kay and I agreed on many, and we argued and compromised on others. The debate got heated at times, but we modeled the behavior that we teach to teams about having a vigorous, productive disagreement to learn through the process. A great debate is never personal, and there is no winner and loser if the debaters have the common goal to emerge with the best idea. The arguing becomes something you laugh about afterward.

The nine nominations that we selected for interviews were:

- ▶ Time Guides – Tour guides would take tourists to witness historic events in the past
- ▶ Making Cryogenics Obsolete – Become the safer alternative to cryogenics for the future
- ▶ Manufacture Timeports for Sale – Timeport to be operated by customers to enable their development of business opportunities to enhance the value of their business
- ▶ Cycle Time and Quality Improvements – Going back in time to observe a business process in the past

to make recommendations for improvement going forward
- Generational Family Reunions – Bring deceased ancestors to the current time for a family reunion
- Relationship Fixer – Going back in time to fix a relationship such as siblings not talking to each other or a girlfriend you should have married
- Timeport 2.0 – An internal business opportunity to upgrade the technology to the next generation to double the rate of vortal acceleration and thus double the number of years it will take a potential competitor to catch up
- Space Travel Acceleration – Use of the time tunnels to reduce time in space from years to seconds
- Video Biographies – Using time travel to film key events in a person's life to make a personal video biography

CHAPTER 19

OPENING THE CAN OF WORMS

MARCUS CAME UP WITH THE great idea for the men to have dinner out and then go to an event. On the skycar ride to the restaurant, my curiosity got the better of me. "I have so many questions, and since you are all a captive audience…." I glanced around, and Sam said, "Shoot."

"I'm mainly wondering how it was decided who would be CEO after you, Sam. Marcus, you and Karena both seem like great leaders…."

Sam interrupted me before I could finish. "When it was time for me to step down, Marcus and Karena bought 80 percent of UST from me. I don't want to speak for my kids, but this time of transition caused some turmoil between Marcus and Karena. Both believed they were qualified and ready to take on the job of CEO. This was before Timeport came on the scene. I wanted this settled before I agreed to the sale of 80 percent of my ownership of UST. Marcus and Karena both lobbied for me to select them. The more they lobbied, the more they grew apart and resented each other."

Gary jumped in. "It was terrible. Marcus and Karena weren't talking to each other. That was the year we didn't spend Thanksgiving together."

Marcus took the story from there. "Both of us resented Dad for not picking either of us."

Sam added, "I finally realized that it was going to be their company, and I needed to get out of the way so they could work it out. I've always believed that conflict can best be resolved through direct, honest conversations."

Marcus said, "Dad was very wise. He knew this was about the characteristic in the TeamScene model called BELIEVE in Each Other. Karena focused our conversation on what we shared that was most important—our family, our childhood, our common values, and our desire for UST to continue its success. We had a frank discussion about our strengths and weaknesses. I think we both felt very vulnerable because we had many years of experience to use against each other. In the end, this was not about sibling rivalry. It was about who could deliver the best returns on our investments in UST. I was a true technician, and she was a natural leader. I took myself out of the running, and it was the best decision of my life. I am so proud of my sister, and I'm glad she is leading this company."

CHAPTER 20

DINNERTIME

Marcus, Sam, Gary, and I had dinner at a great restaurant that served Andorian ribs. I learned that Andoria was a region on Mars named after a husband and wife team of space explorers who were first on that region of the planet. Their names were Andrew and Loria Wilston. Andorian ribs really had nothing to do with Mars, but the ribs were flavored in a dry red spicy powder that looked like the soil on Mars and had a unique taste that really grew on you.

During dinner, Marcus had a question for me. "I've read a lot about the 1960s. What was it like growing up in that era? It sounded like a transformative time in our nation's history in so many ways."

"I guess it was," I said. "The Beatles coming on the scene, watching the perfect families on our new color televisions, Neil Armstrong stepping foot on the moon, hippies openly taking drugs and protesting the Vietnam War, and the Dodgers and Yankees battling it out in the World Series."

"I want to know what it was like for *you* growing up in the 1960s," Marcus clarified.

I paused to let the memories wash over me. "The 1960s were an interesting time to be a kid. I still have this notion, born of that era, that most people are well intentioned and want a country that is patriotic and free. Television shows shaped a lot of thinking during that decade. Those shows had story lines where the families stuck together, the parents told their kids to do what was right, and the kids respected their parents. But that was in stark contrast to what was happening in some parts of the nation. On one hand, the decade was almost idyllic, and on the other hand, it was very volatile. President Kennedy and Martin Luther King were assassinated. Young people were protesting the war and what they called the Establishment—the business world and government. There were riots. The primarily white-dominated culture was beginning to change, but not without some growing pains. I remember not wanting to hear about all the riots and the political uprisings. I just wanted to watch those TV shows with idealistic story lines and listen to my favorite Los Angeles sports teams on the radio."

Everyone had stopped eating, absorbed in listening as I reminisced. "Baseball was my favorite sport, and I played Little League. In those days, kids played outside with each other. All the neighborhood boys and I played baseball and touch football in the street and basketball in one of our driveways. Sports definitely shaped my thinking about teamwork, both the social aspect of sports and the competitive aspect.

When I play baseball now, in 2016, I still enjoy the social outlet it provides. You know, what gets discussed in the dugout stays in the dugout. And even though I'm in my late fifties, I still want to win every game."

We shared a laugh at that comment, and everyone ordered coffee and dessert.

CHAPTER 21

BATTER UP

As we finished dinner, it was my turn to be curious. I asked, "What are sports like in 2085?"

"Nothing like in your time, Dad," said Sam. "But we are about to find out since Marcus and Gary are treating us to a minor league baseball game played by the local team called the Space City Travelers."

He knew he'd hit a home run with that news when I grinned and said, "Yes! I've been wanting to watch some baseball in 2085."

When we arrived at the ballpark, I realized that baseball was nothing like it was in my time. The field looked mostly the same, but the stadium was quite different. The seats were bigger and more comfortable, like recliners. There were no concession stands since each seat had its own food replicator kind of like in *Star Trek* in the 1960s. Marcus told me that food replicators were really just 3D printers using food ingredients instead of plastics. He also explained that there were not as many seats in the stadium as there used to be because many people enjoyed the game in the comfort of their home. Those who attended the live event did so for a luxury experience.

Before the game started, Sam announced to Marcus and Gary, "You know, my dad took me to my first baseball game when I was a one-year-old in 1998. It was at the Houston Astrodome, and we went with my dad's friend John and his teenage son Tim. I actually don't remember much other than my dad telling me when I was older that I was sitting on his lap and kept reaching my hand back to my dad and saying 'Mama.'"

When the Space City Travelers game started, I realized there was something missing. "Where are the umpires?" I asked, utterly baffled.

Sam laughed. "You're so old-fashioned, Dad. I love it. Everything is new to you. It's great." He explained, "Umpires became unnecessary as technology advanced. Each player now has sensors throughout his uniform so the technology umpire makes the call. For example, on a player stealing second base, if the fielder's glove or baseball touches the stealing player before he gets to the base as determined by the base sensor, then the technology umpire calls an out—up there on the scoreboard. Also, Dad, you may not have noticed that the center fielder is a she. We have had women in baseball for quite some time now. Not many, but there are some."

Gary said, "Don't forget to use these." He handed me a pair of glasses that looked like a cross between virtual reality headsets and 3D glasses. "You can use these to watch your own instant replay or get customized statistics," he explained. "You can also plug these ear pieces in to get your own audio announcer for the game. If it's coded to the beginner setting, the spectator gets a lot of very basic education about the game in progress, and a knowledgeable spectator gets expert analysis about the game."

It was great watching a baseball game in 2085. Despite all the advancements, it was still baseball. Whether in my time or in 2085, all feels right with the world when you are at a baseball game.

When the game ended, Gary couldn't resist telling me, "If you think baseball has changed, wait until I tell you about football."

On the drive back to Gary's house, he told me how football was no longer played on the field anymore because of the concussions so many players had suffered in the past. Football had become what we call virtual reality. Each player was stationed in his own room making the same movements as in traditional football but using 3D technology. A passer still had to pass the ball using the same motion. An offensive lineman still had to engage the defensive lineman to keep the opposing player from getting to the quarterback. The difference was that there was no physical contact, just virtual 3D contact displayed in 3D arenas or a home theater. Because the technology was so good, it looked like you were seeing actual players blocking and tackling. It would probably take some getting used to for me, but the 2085 football fan couldn't imagine players getting hurt like they did in my time.

When we arrived at Gary's house, I thanked Marcus and Sam. "As fun as the surprise party was, this was my favorite night of the trip. I not only got to see a baseball game in 2085, but I spent an enjoyable evening with my son, my grandson and my grandson-in-law. I wish I could say that this is a night I will never forget…."

CHAPTER 22

The Reason We Are Here

During the next phase of the Teamwork Sharks process, Kay and I conducted interviews of the nominees we selected. When they submitted their nominations, Kay and I learned about each business opportunity, the business case for the idea, and why this idea could only be achieved by working well as a team. Now, in the interview stage of the process, we wanted to know more about:

- ▶ The purpose of the business opportunity
- ▶ The nominator's passion for the idea
- ▶ The nominator's readiness to be the leader of this opportunity
- ▶ Any obstacles they might face implementing it
- ▶ How well they articulated their case
- ▶ How they responded to challenging questions.

Karena and Marcus explained to Kay and me prior to this phase that the reason they wanted us to do the Teamwork

Sharks (in addition to the family connection) instead of doing it themselves was our ability to think strategically to utilize our business/financial acumen, and our experience as independent business advisors. With my accounting background, enterprise/cross-functional business advisory capabilities, leadership coaching, and expertise as a teamwork engineer, and Kay's experience in engineering, strategy consulting, and collaboration in driving stronger enterprise results, we brought some unique capabilities to a unique opportunity—Timeport.

The interviews were our opportunity to separate the great ideas from the good ones so that the great ones could be tested in an atmosphere of competition and constructive challenges at the Teamwork Sharks event. The very best would flourish and rise to the top of the list.

CHAPTER 23

THE MIGHT TO REUNITE

KAY AND I WERE EXTREMELY impressed with the people we interviewed at UST.

We came into the interview for Ray Wong's Time Guides business opportunity believing it had tremendous potential. Based on our one concern, however, we challenged him on the ability to keep from changing the future. His answer gave us the confidence to consider his idea for the Teamwork Sharks event.

Another business opportunity worth considering was that of Sarah Serromaya, a first-year human resources representative. When Sarah came into the conference room, Kay and I greeted this young, confident future leader.

After a few minutes of getting to know each other, I said to Sarah, "Tell us about this business opportunity."

Sarah had come prepared. "Generational Family Reunions would work similarly to how it happened for you when you came here from 2016. Our team of family tree researchers would work with the current family members to gather information about the ancestor. Karena and Marcus knew a lot about you and Sam when they arrived in your time. Your reaction that it was a hoax was natural, and probably very typical to how most people would react. The historian and the wardrobe consultant would work as a team to research the place, time, and customs of the period when the ancestor lived so that the time traveler would not look out of place. The landing location would be near the home of the ancestor."

"Our Timeport engineer would arrange the technical quality and safety of the trip. A Timeport reunion expert and one family member would go back to the target date and bring the target ancestors forward in time for the family reunion. Everyone would arrive back at UST headquarters for debriefing. The actual reunion would be at a new facility designed for reunions. In addition to the event facilities, it would have a hotel for all the guests of today and the past. The next day we would provide a guided tour of Space City as well as an on-premises museum to educate the guests of what our current time is like. Security and safety must be of utmost importance, and this would give us greater ability to control the whereabouts of the guests."

Kay asked, "Before we dig deeper into your business opportunity, can you tell us more about yourself, and how someone who is relatively new to business came up with such an intriguing idea?"

Sarah responded, "I grew up with two brothers and a sister in a Southern Arizona town called Rio Rico down from the Santa Rita Mountains. Family has always meant a lot to me. One of my older brothers died when I was eight, and I still miss him fifteen years later. My mother passed away last year. It seems that death has been a bigger part of my life than it has for others my age. I miss my brother and mother, and I want to see them again. I want to bring them into the future so we can have a family reunion. I want this for me. I want this for my father. I want this for my grandmother. I want this for my living brother and sister. But I also want as many people as possible to be able to reunite with their loved ones."

I was impressed. "You clearly have a passion for this idea, but why is it a good business opportunity for UST?"

Sarah seemed ready for this question. "As you know, from the financial projections in my nomination, this would be highly profitable for us. I would be happy to go through the numbers, but at a summary level, UST would generate $200 billion in revenue in the first year. That's one hundred times more than our core business. We also would deliver $180 billion in profit."

Kay and I glanced at each other and nodded. Those were huge profits indeed.

Sarah continued. "But if profits are not the only factor in this competition, then we as a company need to consider what our purpose is for Timeport. What greater purpose could there be than to reconnect lost family members? We can be influential in helping families stay together. This will help young people get the wise advice and guidance they need from their elders in this changing world. I know I am thinking idealistically, but family is at the core of any society, so a stronger family should strengthen our culture at its core. I believe UST can make a lot of money with Generational Family Reunions, but we can also change society for the better."

Kay was ready to ask a question, but Sarah interrupted her because she seemed very determined to make a point. "Kay, my apologies for interrupting but I want to ask Mike a few questions. You're having a family reunion right now. Is this a life experience that you would never trade even though you are not going to remember it? Do you think being here is going to have a positive impact on your 2085 family? If you knew this could be possible, would you allocate money for this purpose by putting some away in trust now, in your time, for use in the future by your descendants?"

Kay jumped in before I could answer. "If it were me, my answers would be yes, yes, and yes. This is an awesome experience for Mike and his family. I hope I will have this opportunity some day with my family. I just wish Mike's wife, Pam, could be here. I hope she will have this opportunity soon."

Sarah smiled at such a positive response. "I never would have thought of this if Karena and Marcus hadn't brought you guys here. That opened up all sorts of possibilities, and when I heard about this competition, the creative ideas just came together."

"It is kind of amazing, isn't it?" I said.

Kay's brows creased in a frown. "I do have a concern. Your plan is to do a thousand family reunions a year. That is about three per day. That seems like a lot. How would you be able to make that happen safely and efficiently?"

Sarah seemed unfazed by the question. In fact, she seemed to know that this question was coming. I had a startling thought. Maybe this was the second time she had heard the question. Maybe she had used Timeport to go back in time to answer it now more effectively. *This time travel stuff is getting to me*, I thought. I turned off the irrational, skeptical voice in my head and listened to her confident response. "The plan is to have ten cross-functional project teams that will each have the following team members:

- A historian to help us with researching the conditions/culture at the destination
- A geographist who helps us point Timeport to the safest location
- A wardrobe specialist to help us with clothes that blend in with the time period
- An explorer to accompany the time traveler to the destination to bring the ancestor back for the reunion
- An engineer to execute the Timeport procedures from UST
- An event planner for the reunion
- A family coordinator to work with the family in 2085, or whatever year it happens to be
- A healthcare specialist to screen and treat the explorer and time traveler for harmful viruses/bacteria before they go back in time to the past

"Each project team would be assigned to a project for two weeks that would include research, going back in time, the reunion, and returning the family member to their own time period. In addition, a coordinator would be assigned for each of the roles listed above to oversee excellence. For example, an individual would coordinate the historians for all ten project teams to have common procedures, establish best practices, hire and fire the historians, and so on. That coordinator would work with the other coordinators to ensure they are providing consistent leadership cross functionally.

"Our greatest costs would be the personnel cost of the team, the cost to operate Timeport, and the cost of the reunion event. Total cost would be $40 million per project, not much considering that the revenue from the project will be about ten times that.

"It will take a well-oiled operation, but we can make this work. It is important to be able to serve as many families as we can."

Kay and I were impressed. I responded, "Sarah, you have really thought this through. We are impressed. But as a CPA and a former auditor, I think I may have you on something. I noticed that you are planning a thousand annual family reunions at $400 million each, which is a total of $400 billion, yet the revenue in your nomination is only $200 billion. Is there a miscalculation?"

Sarah laughed. "There is no miscalculation. I am proposing that UST match the number of paid reunions with free scholarship reunions for those who can't afford it. Look, it's the right thing to do. People should have the opportunity to meet their ancestors even if they don't have $400 million. UST deserves to make a great profit from Timeport, but if we get greedy and don't give back, the government will take this from us in taxes anyway. From the beginning, we need to consider our market perception and how we will be seen by the government and regulators."

I had one more question. "You're pretty new to business and UST. What makes you think you could pull this off and be able to lead a cross-functional team effort with people who are a lot more experienced than you?"

Sarah didn't flinch. "I would want the job of leading this team even if I wasn't paid a red cent, using an expression from back in your time. In addition to my passion, in my short time here at UST, I have gained a lot of respect from those experienced people I might be leading. I am very conscientious about doing it right the first time and every time after that. I am very straightforward with people and let them know what my expectations are of them. I am not afraid to have a conversation with them if they are not meeting my expectations. Even though I am a young woman, I am told that I am wise beyond my years, and I never let my emotions get the better of me. I believe I am ready to lead the Generational Family Reunions team."

Kay then closed the interview. "Thank you, Sarah, for your time. Your idea is awesome, and you are awesome. You will find out soon if you will be a finalist for the Teamwork Sharks event."

When Sarah left, I said to Kay, "Meeting someone like Sarah gives me hope for this world and this galaxy. Her spirit is infectious. She has the potential to be a great leader."

Kay agreed. "Too bad we can't go forward in time to see what she becomes."

Over the next couple of days, we completed our interviews of all nine nominations. It was not going to be an easy decision to select four presenters, but that was our next task. The decisions keep getting tougher because the business opportunities keep getting better.

CHAPTER 24

MISSING PAM

ONE EVENING THAT WEEK, IT occurred to me that I hadn't talked to my wife Pam in about three weeks. It felt strange when I realized that she didn't even know I was gone.

I had really been missing her, though, and not being able to tell her about this amazing experience felt disorienting. I wished she could be here to experience this with me. She would so enjoy seeing what had become of our son and his family. She would be so proud.

It then became clear that I was experiencing the value of a family reunion. I realized that I truly understood the value of the Family Reunions business opportunity in ways that no one else at UST could because I was experiencing its positive impact right now. As a Teamwork Shark, I also had to remain objective and not let my own personal emotions overtake the rational assessment that I needed to make of Sarah's business plan.

Then it came to me. In exchange for our free-of-charge consulting, I wanted a commitment that no matter what business opportunity Kay and I chose, UST would bring Pam to 2085 to meet our extended family in the future. I didn't know when that might be possible, but I knew I would be happy knowing that it would happen.

I went to find Karena. She was in the kitchen. I asked her if she would commit to doing this. I wanted to know that it would happen. She looked at me and gave me a big hug. "Of course, Grandpa. Remember, I was young when she died. I miss Grandma too."

CHAPTER 25

AND THE FINALISTS ARE...

Karena sounded very excited when she kicked off the meeting with all company personnel in attendance either in person or by video link.

"This is a big day for us. Mike and Kay are going to announce the finalists. We are one step closer to positively transforming the human experience. I want to thank all of you who submitted nominations and who have been part of our team to help us do something special for so many people from many generations. None of this would be possible without the vision of my dad who helped make time travel a reality." Karena got a little emotional. "Marcus and I have been able to meet our grandfather. Yes, this is a business, but we're about to have a transformative effect on the human experience. We have a great responsibility to do this right. Without further ado, let's bring Mike and Kay up here to announce the finalists."

I spoke first. "I just want you all to know how grateful Kay and I are to be here. A few weeks ago, my son Sam was nineteen and a freshman in college. I am very proud to see that my son's work is now impacting society in a way that no parent could ever imagine. Meeting my grandchildren and their grandchildren has been the most special experience of my life. It is an unbelievable honor that Kay and I were asked to be of help here. We have taken our responsibility seriously. These business opportunities are going to change people's lives. Kay is now going to announce the finalists."

"We had nine great nominations, and the interviews made it difficult to choose one," Kay began. "Those of you who were not selected as finalists, I want to encourage you to come talk to us and find out why we did not select you. In some situations, the business case may not have been strong enough. At every selection round, we made our decision based on the business case that offered the best, biggest, and most probable business opportunity. And now we will announce the four finalists."

The crowd murmured with excitement. For many in the audience, this was the first they had heard about these business opportunities.

"The first finalist is Time Guides," Kay continued. "The Time Guide would be a tour guide who takes tourists back in time to witness a historic event. Let's congratulate Ray Wong, the leader of the Mission Planning unit, on his fantastic idea and flawless business proposal. Great job, Ray."

Kay paused for some loud applause, and a female voice from the crowd yelled, "I love you, Ray!"

"Sounds like Ray has an admirer," Kay said before she continued. "Our next finalist is Evangelina Walker, the

Director of Environmental Safety. The business opportunity she proposed was to Make Cryogenics Obsolete and to capture as much of the cryogenics market as possible. Instead of being frozen before death through cryogenics, customers would prepay for their descendants or future guardian to bring them from a designated year in the past to a designated year in the future. This would accomplish the same goal as cryogenics but be much safer, and the customer would not have to be frozen prematurely in their own time before death. How about a hand for Evangelina?"

Based on the cheering, it was clear that either the idea or Evangelina were a fan favorite.

Kay continued. "Mike and I really enjoyed talking to our next finalist. Sarah Serromaya is a first-year human resources representative. The business opportunity she proposed is not only a potential moneymaker, but it could have quite a positive impact on the fabric of the family. Her proposal is called Generational Family Reunions. Sarah's idea is being pilot tested right now with Mike, Sam, Karena, Marcus, and their families.

"As you probably know by now, Mike and I came here from 2016 using your Timeport technology, and Mike has been able to meet his descendants, something neither of us ever would have dreamed possible. We have a special affinity to this idea because we're living it right now, but we are committed to considering it objectively in relation to the others.

"We know most of you would want to experience a generational family reunion. I am sure the audience already has an opinion as to whether this will be the best, biggest, and most probable business opportunity of the nine nominations." The crowd let their opinions be known with their cheering.

Kay was ready to introduce the last finalist. "Last but not least is finalist number four." A hush fell over the crowd as everyone wondered whether their favorite business opportunity had been selected.

"Benjamin Morgan, the Manager of Analytics, proposes accelerating space travel through Timeport," Kay continued. "Currently, as you know, it takes one and a half years using today's propulsion to reach Saturn. Benjamin's proposal is called Space Travel Acceleration. The travelers would reach their destination in space instantaneously using a reverse Timeport technology by residents already in that location. Benjamin is ready to make the case that although it will cannibalize some of our core business, the overall effect will be positive."

Someone yelled out, "But isn't that the same thing as using Timeport to go to the future? That could be a risk for changing the future."

"Great question and comment," Kay replied. "There will be an opportunity for each of you to participate, ask questions, and challenge the finalists at the Teamwork Sharks event. For now, let's congratulate Benjamin Morgan for being a finalist." It was a nice round of applause, but I was glad to hear that there was going to be some healthy debate and engagement by all.

And the Finalists Are...

I stood up and waited until I had everyone's attention. "You will be hearing soon about the Teamwork Sharks event schedule. We want as many of you to attend as possible while still providing excellent service to your customers. Kay and I would like to meet with the finalists first thing in the morning in the Milky Way Conference Room to help you get ready for the Teamwork Sharks event."

CHAPTER 26

Empathizing with God

You could see the excitement on some of the finalists' faces when they walked into the Milky Way Conference Room that morning. These weren't just typical ideas for improving their business operations. These opportunities would transform the human experience.

Before the official start of the meeting, Sarah Serromaya asked me a question that made everyone in the room stop talking. "What if we haven't planned for all the consequences, and we end up disturbing historic events? If we change history, that will change our world today. We might cause ourselves not to exist, or we might make the world an even more dangerous place."

She had created an opening to let others voice their concerns.

Ray Wong asked, "What if the Timeport technology gets in the wrong hands?"

It was Evangelina Walker's turn. "What if those from the past who come to our time end up remembering 2085 when they return to their time?"

Karena stood up, looking very confident as if she was ready for these questions. "This is beginning to settle in for all of us. We have a monumental responsibility to do this right and to make it safe. There could be dire consequences if we mess this up. I wonder if God ever felt this way. If so, I can totally empathize right now. The human experiment and the Timeport experiment are not without risks. But let's remember what impact we might be able to make. Sarah, you might be able to see your brother for the first time since he died. Ray, you might be able to take a quick trip to Saturn and be back the same day. Evangelina, you love to travel and learn about history. Imagine what you could learn first-hand through Time Guides. We need to take the risks seriously, but we have an opportunity to do this the right way and protect the safety of people in the past, present, and future. If we cannot do this safely, then we will not go forward—period."

I was proud of my granddaughter. She was definitely a great leader. She was like Pam. She had that natural ability to connect with people and get them motivated.

She had inspired us, and now there was an atmosphere of determination and eagerness in the conference room.

I spoke up and said, "After that wonderful speech by Karena, there's really nothing more for Kay and me to say. The Teamwork Sharks event will be one week from today starting at eight a.m. Each of you will have twenty minutes to present, and there will be twenty minutes for discussion. That discussion will include some challenges from Kay and me but also questions or challenges from your coworkers.

Karena, I assume every employee at UST is welcome as long as customers are taken care of."

"Certainly," she said.

I continued. "Here are some final tips for making your pitch to us:

- ▶ Make your appeal to all stakeholders, not just Kay and me. Although we will make the decision on the winner, we will consider feedback from the executives and the audience.
- ▶ Excite your audience. You can use drama, the element of surprise, or audience involvement.
- ▶ Prioritize your twenty minutes. Too much granular data or a bunch of bullet points will not be a good use of your time. Focus on what distinguishes your business opportunity from the others.
- ▶ Keep it personal. Kay and I want to know what you really think about this and why it means so much to you.
- ▶ Practice, practice, practice. Do a dry run, and you will feel ready and confident when you present.
- ▶ When you are making your presentation, be in the moment and let your instincts take over."

Kay then closed. "Good luck to all of you. Finalists, if you have questions for Mike or me, please do not hesitate to ask."

CHAPTER 27

All Work and No Play

Kay and I left the conference room after the meeting ended. We had some preparations to do to make sure we were on the same page with the agenda for the event, but that was a week away.

I was really enjoying our time in 2085. I didn't want it to end. I thought to myself that we should see Arizona while we were here.

"Kay, why don't we ask Gary if he would show us some sights around Space City?" I said, voicing that thought.

"No can do, Mike. I have plans."

"Plans? You already have friends here in 2085?" I guess I was caught a bit off guard, but it shouldn't have surprised me knowing how friendly and open Kay is.

"I actually have plans with Roberto. He is taking the rest of the day off. We're going to take a drive in the desert and have a picnic."

I remembered the evening with my family when I met my great grandchildren. Roberto volunteered to show Kay around. They were both single, so there was no harm in Kay making friends in 2085.

I thought I would have a little fun with her. "Sounds like there may be some romance brewing here."

Kay responded with a smile and a bit of a twinkle in her eyes. "Mike, to be honest, the romance has already brewed. I think half the people at UST know about it. You're probably the only one who's been in the dark. This is our fourth date!"

I just started laughing—at myself and the situation. Good for her. Why not? Of course, I couldn't resist having some fun with this. "You know, Kay, we are not supposed to have relationships with our clients. And talk about robbing the cradle, you are almost twice his age."

No sooner had I said that than I saw Roberto walking toward us. I turned to Kay and whispered in a mock fatherly way, "Don't let him take advantage of you."

When Roberto walked up, Kay said to him, "Grandpa here finally knows about us."

Roberto gave me a very serious look. "I will have her home before curfew, sir."

CHAPTER 28

STEPPING IN THE BUCKET

ALTHOUGH KAY AND I HAD led quite a few of these Teamwork Shark events, this one was going to be special. We had breakfast that morning at a little coffee shop right near the office to make sure we were on the same page.

The event would take place at a meeting facility nearby that Karena had rented so that everyone at UST could attend. The executives had decided this meeting was important enough to allow as many employees as possible to attend and only have a skeleton crew of staff available to serve customers with urgent needs.

As we were about to enter the auditorium, I smiled at Kay and said, "UST is going to make history today." We walked in the door and saw about a thousand people in attendance, some already in their seats, some standing in clusters in the lobby chatting with their friends. The excitement in their faces was evident.

I was caught a bit off guard when a man stopped us. "Mike, Kay, I would really like your autographs. I have been telling my wife about you, and I thought it would be cool to get your autographs for her." As we walked down the aisle to the front of the auditorium, people kept stopping us to take photos with us and to get our autographs.

Just before we walked up the steps to the stage, I felt a tug on my shirt. It was Benjamin Morgan. He motioned for Kay and me to follow him through the side door. Once we exited the auditorium, I saw the fear on his face. "Kay, Mike—I don't think I can present today. I'm not feeling well. I better not go on that stage. I feel dizzy and nauseous. I'm going to die if I go up there."

"Benjamin, if you are sick or just feeling nervous, and you don't want to go up there, I totally understand. The fear of public speaking is often greater than the fear of dying. You don't need to do this, okay?"

"Okay," Benjamin responded, and he visibly relaxed.

"You know," I said, "this makes me think of a story about Sam when he was nine years old. It taught me a lot. Sam started playing Little League baseball when he was five. For his birthday present when he was seven, we gave him some batting lessons from a former Houston Astros player named Terry Puhl. When Sam was nine, his Little League transitioned from having the players hit the ball pitched by machines to having them hit against the opposing team's nine-year-old pitchers. Because these pitchers weren't very accurate, a lot of the batters developed bad habits out of a fear of being hit by the ball, such as stepping out of the batter's box. In baseball lingo, that's called stepping in the bucket. It throws off all the batters' mechanics, and they rarely hit the ball well."

Kay and Benjamin listened with interest. I continued. "I noticed Sam was stepping out, so I informed Terry Puhl before Sam's batting lesson and asked him to tell Sam to stop doing that. At the lesson, Sam was stepping out, and Terry never mentioned it. I was getting frustrated that Terry wasn't saying anything to him. Terry just started again from scratch with Sam on proper hitting mechanics. He re-taught Sam to execute his swing. He never told him to stop the bad habit, and it worked. Sam never stepped in the bucket again. I learned that day that if someone has a fear that is affecting their performance, don't tell them what NOT to do. Tell them what TO do. Instead of reinforcing the fear by telling Sam what not to do, Terry refocused Sam on what to do by using the best batting approach."

"So what does that have to do with me?" Benjamin asked.

"Benjamin, you don't have to go out there if you don't want to. But if you do, just focus on the great idea that you want to share. Tell us in your own words about the compelling business case for this. Your communication skills are quite good. Just speak to the audience like you are speaking to us right now. Just execute your swing."

Benjamin paused before responding, "Maybe I will…."

Kay said, "You're the last one to present, so when it's your turn, if we don't see you walking toward the stage, we'll make up a reason for why you're unable to present. Does that sound okay?"

Benjamin looked relieved. "Okay, that's fair."

Kay and I made our way back into the auditorium. Kay whispered to me, "Did that really happen with Terry Puhl?"

I just smiled at her and then responded, "You bet it did."

CHAPTER 29

THE KICKOFF

KARENA QUIETED THE CROWD DOWN. "Welcome, everyone! Welcome to the Teamwork Sharks event! Let's get started." She paused to let the audience get completely quiet. "This is a special day for UST, one that we will remember for quite some time. We are about to do something special, and we are glad that you are here to help us get there."

"As you all know, my father, Sam, started this company. Marcus and I are proud that he is our father and feel grateful for the opportunity to enjoy this turning point in human history with him. At eighty-eight years of age, my father is seeing two of his dreams fulfilled: to see his father again and to make time travel a viable, commercial enterprise so that generations of people can get the most out of life without the obstacle of time."

People in the audience spontaneously stood up to give Sam an ovation. Sam reluctantly stood and waved to the crowd, which made them cheer louder.

Karena continued. "Marcus and I and our families are very grateful to meet Mike Goodfriend, our grandfather. We knew our grandmother, Pam, but have never had a chance to meet our grandfather. When Marcus and I met Mike, we could see why our father grew to be such an outstanding man. And more importantly, being able to take advantage of the original Teamwork Sharks, Mike and Kay, is a unique opportunity at a crucial time in our business. So, let me turn over the floor to my grandfather and the originator of the Teamwork Sharks, Mike Goodfriend."

I walked up to the stage accompanied by the song "Carry on My Wayward Son" by Kansas. This was a favorite of mine when I was in college in the 1970s. I don't know how they knew.

This was a special moment for me as I took the microphone, "Karena, thank you for your kind comments. The feeling is very mutual, and it is so great for Kay and me to be here with all of you. For someone that is uncomfortable with the spotlight, I have to say that this feels pretty special. Just like we teach, appreciation means the most when it is genuine and spontaneous."

I waited while the audience responded with a round of applause and a few whistles and cheers. Seems the vintage rock and roll music had the same effect on them as it had on me, and they were primed and ready. "We have a full day today. We have four presentations, each of which will be twenty minutes or less. After that, twenty minutes will be allocated for feedback and questions.

"We also would like your feedback digitally. Use your devices to complete the survey and provide your comments. After all the presentations are finished, Kay and I will summarize the feedback, and you'll be able to see it on the screens as well. We will all break for a working lunch. During that hour, while you enjoy your lunch and review the feedback, Kay and I will have lunch privately to prepare for our questions for the executives.

"Kay and I will award the Teamwork Sharks Tooth Award to the winner. Our goal as the Teamwork Sharks is to help surface the best, biggest, and most probable business opportunity, and to provide our professional expertise in selecting a winner. The executive team will decide which business opportunities go forward. When those business opportunities are funded, a team will need to be formed, and the project will need to be executed effectively as a team.

"So here we go, first up is...."

CHAPTER 30

Time Guides

Ray Wong started his presentation by asking a question to the audience. "What historical event do you believe shaped us as we are today?"

One person yelled out, "Signing of the Declaration of Independence."

"Thanks Brennan. What if I told you that you could go back in time and observe the events leading up to it?"

Brennan responded, "If it was safe for me, then it would be the experience of a lifetime because our lives and our ancestors' lives would have been very different without those brave signers. Many people considered them traitors to the king of England, and their lives were at risk by signing their names. It would give me a new appreciation for the freedoms we enjoy."

With that as a great lead-in to his presentation, Ray explained his idea for Time Guides. He was masterful at involving the audience and drawing upon their emotions about history. After he went through the impossible-to-match financial data, I realized it was going to be difficult to keep an open mind about the other presentations.

After Ray's presentation and a standing ovation, the audience was very quiet while they entered their feedback.

Several audience members asked Ray about the safety and security challenges of not disturbing the historic events. He answered them calmly and rationally.

Before Ray's time was up, Kay challenged him by asking, "I think you know that we believe you have a great business opportunity. I do have a concern. I believe there is a major risk to filming these historical events. It could cannibalize your own Time Guide revenue as it may cause customers to increasingly watch the film instead of going back in time to observe the actual event. The revenue from the time travel is much more than the revenue from the film views. What are your thoughts on this?"

Ray paused to think about this for a minute. "Kay, that is a great question. I don't have an answer for you on that right now."

I liked his honesty, but it was probably not the best way to end his presentation.

CHAPTER 31

MAKING CRYOGENICS OBSOLETE

EVANGELINA WALKER BEGAN HER PRESENTATION with a body builder carrying a tub of ice onto the stage. She placed chicken meat into the ice and asked the audience what would happen to the meat.

One person yelled out, "It will extend how long you can keep the meat fresh so that it doesn't spoil."

"That's what cryogenics does," said Evangelina, as if she had orchestrated this response. "It extends someone's life until a later time when the person is thawed and woken up, so to speak. But there are problems with cryogenics, just as there can be with ice. If it melts, the meat will spoil. If a cryogenics machine malfunctions for whatever reason, the person will die. Plus, with cryogenics, there is no going back.

"Kay, just think if you had cryogenics in your time, and you decided to freeze yourself for 2085. You would not be able to go back unless you used Timeport, and if you did, there would have been no need for cryogenics in the first place. A person could make a $2 million commitment before they die and tell us what year they want to awaken from their deep-freeze sleep. In that future time, someone from UST would go back in time using Timeport and bring them forward in time."

When Evangelina finished, Kay challenged her thinking. "Evangelina, you did a great job with this, and we do think it is a fantastic business opportunity. One question I have is about the customer's commitment. Would the customer pay the $2 million up front, or would it go into escrow until the time travel event took place?"

Evangelina responded very confidently. "Kay, I know it sounds like they are paying $2 million up front, and UST has use of those funds until the time travel event, which could be twenty, fifty, or even a hundred years into the future. But that's not really the case since the time travel event into the future will happen in the customer's life almost immediately after the customer commitment is made."

"Okay, I understand where you're coming from," said Kay, "but if you test marketed this concept, potential customers would probably feel like UST was taking advantage of the time use of their money."

Kay's scrutiny of this idea was exactly what we try to accomplish in the Teamwork Sharks. This was a great example of a very good business opportunity with real possibilities for success and profit, but Kay and I could only pick one winner, one that we believed would showcase the best, biggest, and most probable business opportunity. We needed to fully vet these opportunities and consider the emotional, market, operational, and financial factors. Kay did a great job of challenging Evangelina on this issue.

Many in the audience seemed to agree with Kay's concern. One audience member also raised a concern that if you put the money in escrow, the customer could structure it so their descendants could pick another provider that, by that time, might be offering the same service.

CHAPTER 32

Generational Family Reunions

Sarah Serromaya had a very serious look about her when she began. "I'm a little bit nervous. I have not done much speaking in front of groups, let alone a group this large." She took a breath as if strengthening her resolve, and when she continued speaking, her tone was confident. "My business opportunity is Generational Family Reunions, and for me, this is personal. I am twenty-three years old. I grew up in southern Arizona in a town called Rio Rico. My older brother died fifteen years ago when he was hit by a car. I miss him every day. My mother just passed away last year at the young age of forty-five. She died of complications from elective surgery."

I looked at the audience and saw how she had touched them with her story. They waited, eager to hear more.

"I also realize this is about business. There are many people like me who have lost loved ones, who would pay any amount to see them again. My projection is that we can serve a thousand families annually by bringing one of their family members from the past to the current time to be at a family reunion at a controlled location. Based on some survey data about what families would pay to keep family members alive, I believe $400 million per reunion is an achievable price, and we don't expect our costs per reunion to be more than $40 million. I am also proposing that five hundred of those reunions be at no charge, and the other half will still deliver $200 billion in annual revenue. There is more to this business opportunity than profit."

She looked across the stage to where I sat next to Kay at a table. Sarah stretched her arm out toward me and said, "Ladies and gentlemen, we are seeing the first Generational Family Reunion with Mike, Sam, Karena, Marcus, and their families. I am so happy for them to be able to meet Mike and spend quality time with him. Karena and Marcus had never met their grandfather until Timeport brought him into the future.

"It has been my mission since we were told about the Teamwork Sharks process to do whatever it takes to present the best business case possible so the executives will select this business opportunity to implement. It is not because I want recognition, and it is not because UST will make a lot of money from this line of business. It's because I want to see my mother and brother again. Thank you!"

The auditorium went from being so quiet you could hear a pin drop to an eruption of cheers that was deafening.

After the cheering finally died down, a young male audience member asked, "Sarah, how will you award the free-of-charge reunions?"

"Our implementation team would need to define those criteria clearly," Sarah answered. "I believe that in addition to financial need, we would need to consider the potential positive impact on the family or society of today. For example, some families are devastated by a sudden death. The emotional damage can continue for generations. A reunion that can reverse that downward family trajectory could be well worth our investment."

Kay had a question for Sarah. "You have made a great business case. My greatest concern is for you. You are twenty-three years old, and you have your whole life in front of you. I know you are passionate about this, but I am fearful that you will either burn out or become a workaholic. Either one would not be good for you or Timeport. What do you have to say about that?"

Sarah gave a lighthearted laugh, much like she did during the interview when we thought we caught her on a miscalculation. "Kay, I appreciate your concern. This is something my mother would be saying to me if she were here. This is a passion for me, but it has to be much bigger than me. Yes, I will work very hard on this, but I can't do it all. I realize that I need to infuse my team with my passion and commitment, or we will fail. I will not let that happen. I know how important it will be for my team members and me to reunite with our families. I want this for other families too." Sarah paused and seemed to be weighing something in her mind. Finally, she said, "Kay, have you ever overly committed your time toward something that is bigger than you are?"

"Yes, I have," said Kay. "Good point."

I looked at Kay. We were on the same page. There was no need to ask any further questions. We had seen what we wanted to see.

CHAPTER 33

SPACE TRAVEL ACCELERATION

As Benjamin Morgan made his way to the stage, he winked at Kay and me. I interpreted that wink as a thank you. He started his presentation with a question.

"What do people value most in life?"

The answers he expected came quickly.

"Love and family," said one person.

"Yes," replied Benjamin. "What's another one?"

"Money—so you can buy happiness," an audience member said to get a few laughs.

Benjamin played along. "I could have a lot of fun with all the money in the world. I am thinking of one more that, without this, the other two are not likely to happen."

One person yelled out, "Chocolate?"

Benjamin replied, "Although chocolate is important, that isn't what I was thinking of."

Sam must have sensed people were getting punchy, so he yelled out the answer. "Time! Without time, none of the others, even chocolate, can be enjoyed."

"Exactly," Benjamin replied. "It takes about one and a half years to travel to Saturn, which is twice as fast as it would have taken in Mike Goodfriend's time. Imagine if space travel was instantaneous, by using Timeport. Not only would this save one and a half years of space travel, but it would also make spaceships unnecessary, thus eliminating the safety risks of traveling through space."

When someone raised his hand, Benjamin answered his question before he had a chance to ask it. "I know what you are thinking. This is going to cannibalize our existing market for our core services—mission planning, astronaut services, in-flight meals, communication and entertainment, as well as spacecraft storage, fueling, and maintenance. Was that what you wanted to say?"

The person nodded, so Benjamin finished his thought. "You are right. It will. Since the travel through Timeport will be approximately three times the revenue for the associated UST services at a comparable cost, this is a profitable business opportunity. We expect to serve ten times the number of customers through UST, because many of them will choose Timeport over traditional space travel."

He paused to let the murmured discussion among the audience members die down before he continued.

"Although the financial benefits of this business opportunity don't approach some of the others presented, this one is highly profitable because it enhances our advantage over our competitors who provide the same core services. Thank you for the opportunity to present this to you, and to take a swing at the Teamwork Sharks Tooth Award."

The applause from the audience was polite. I didn't sense a lot of excitement in the crowd, and even if the other businesses hadn't presented such great cases with tremendous financial opportunities, I would have been very supportive of moving forward with this one.

The mood in the auditorium seemed somber. Was it just that people were hungry and ready for lunch, or were they collectively dispirited? I turned to the audience and said, "Does anyone have any concerns about this business opportunity?"

A woman stood up and said, "My name is Carrie. Benjamin Morgan is one of the smartest people I know at UST. Space Travel Acceleration is probably a good opportunity for the future of this company, but I am a single mother, and I am feeling uncertain. A UST that no longer needs to provide its core services might not need me, and I will be out of a job."

I looked at Benjamin and feared that this would trigger his anxiety to return. He looked down to collect his thoughts, and then answered in a calm, assured tone. "I recently read a great book written back in Mike Goodfriend's time around 2005. It was called *Our Iceberg Is Melting* by John Kotter and Holger Rathgeber. It was a story about penguins living on an iceberg that was melting. Most of the penguins didn't want to believe that it was melting, and they couldn't accept that they would have to move to another iceberg. We humans tend to have the same mentality. In the case of UST, when other time travel competitors come on the scene, that will be a signal to us that our core services iceberg is melting. Our customers keep coming back to UST because of how all of you in this audience have served their space travel needs. Even in the face of radical change in this industry, many of our customers will continue to use spaceships as their preferred method of transportation across the solar system. Space Travel Acceleration ensures that we keep serving those customers over the long term if our iceberg melts."

Benjamin just looked at the crowd without saying a word. After a few moments of silence, during which he wondered if his message had hit home, the crowd went crazy. That answer clearly resonated with them.

Kay jumped in. "Time's up for Benjamin. Mike and I believe you have helped us all consider the strategic fit for a Timeport business opportunity—to increase UST's advantage through the integration of its core business with any new business from Timeport. We have now heard four great presentations. Get your feedback in, everyone. After lunch, Mike and I will talk with the executives here on the stage to get their thoughts about these business opportunities. Food is being served next door in the ballroom. Enjoy your lunch, and we'll see you in an hour."

CHAPTER 34

A Working Lunch

Kay and I stayed in the auditorium and had some lunch delivered to us while we prepared for the open meeting with the executives. While we were eating, I started thinking out loud. "You know, we'll probably return to 2016 soon. I'm not sure I'm ready."

"Okay, we can't think about that right now," said Kay. "Let's figure out what we are going to ask the execs. I think the winner should be…."

"Hold on," I said, interrupting her. "We can talk about the winners later. Right now, we need to think about the questions we want to ask the executives that will help us make the decision without making this their decision. Remember that after the Teamwork Sharks event, the executives will choose which business opportunity will go forward. Our job is to determine, in our judgment, the best, biggest, and most probable cross-functional business opportunity that can be achieved only by working well as a team. They are depending on us as independent advisors to assess the business cases utilizing our expertise in strategy, leadership, finance, process, and engineering. So let's come up with some questions. Remember, the questions we ask and the answers they give will be instructive to the audience members both in what they say and what they don't say."

Kay and I took a few minutes to think about what we should ask. I interrupted the silence and suggested, "Let's just ask the execs to quickly describe what they liked and disliked about each of the business opportunities."

Kay's mathematical mind started working. "Okay, let's figure out how long this might take. There are eight execs, and if each takes fifteen minutes, it will take two hours for them all to speak. We don't have that much time. Instead, I would like to know how important it is for the business opportunity to be an extension or to be synergistic with the core business services that UST already provides. I am also interested in what each executive sees as the relative importance of the key criteria, such as profit, safety, and the impact on society."

"Okay, I can go along with that," I said. "I want to know if there is such a thing as too much or too little profit based on their expectations. I would also like them to tell me what would be a showstopper when it comes to the criteria, something that would cause them to reject that idea."

Lunch was over, and people were streaming into the auditorium. I looked at my watch. We only had ten minutes before we met with the execs.

CHAPTER 35

Executive Session

Kay and I took our positions to one side of the podium while the execs took their seats on bar stools on the opposite side of the small stage, arranged in a semi-circle facing us. Each of the executives came up and shook our hands. First was Roberto Rodriguez, the VP of Galactic Strategy. (I noticed he gave Kay a different smile than he gave me.) After him was Shannon Block, the Chief Marketing Officer, then Rory Williams, the Chief Operations Officer; Dianne Ferrini, the CFO; Martina Bryan, the VP of Technology; Rashad Ford, the VP of Sales, and Karena.

I whispered to Karena, "Should we wait a few minutes for Marcus?"

She whispered into my ear, "No, you better not. He had to take Sam somewhere, and I am not sure if he will be back in time to join us. No big problem with Sam ... uh ... well ... sometimes older people have little accidents—you know what I mean, right?"

I whispered, "The secret is safe with me."

I kicked things off. "Thanks again to the four presenters who did a great job." The crowd applauded. "This afternoon, we will ask the executives key questions pertaining to each business opportunity so that we can all learn what they believe is important from a strategic point of view. We will not ask them which presentation they would pick, and execs, we prefer that you not share that information with us so we can remain objective. Before Kay asks the first question, you probably have noticed that Marcus is missing. He is with Sam right now, and both of them should be returning later."

It was Kay's turn to speak. "Not all the business opportunities are closely linked to the UST core services supporting space travel. Is it important to the executive team for Timeport to be an extension of your core services or at least synergistic with those services?"

Karena looked at Roberto who stood up to answer. "It would be nice if, all things being equal, it was an extension of our core galactic services, but this is not a requirement of the executive team, and clearly these opportunities are not equal."

Kay replied, "That raises a question for me. You have stated that the success criteria for a Timeport business opportunity must include the amount of profit, safety for all both past and present, no environmental time garbage, has a positive impact on society, and does not alter history. If you were to weight those five criteria, how would you weight them?"

Two executives wanted to speak. Dianne Ferrini spoke first. "I'm not sure I can weight them, but I can rank them.

You might be surprised by my answer since I am the CFO. I believe not altering history is most important followed by safety for all, no 2085 garbage left behind in the past, then profit, and finally, positive impact on society."

All the executives nodded in agreement, including Rory Williams, who had been planning to answer until Dianne answered for the entire executive team.

I asked, "Can there be too much profit?" I let them think about this for a moment. "And on the flip side, what is not enough profit?"

The executives looked everywhere but at me. They were silent for what seemed like eternity. Maybe I was speaking a different language, or maybe Timeport had malfunctioned so I was now speaking the language of an alien from another planet.

Karena spoke up. "That is a very difficult question. I don't think any of us have ever had to consider whether we are making too much profit. Luckily, we still conduct business in a free market system here in 2085, although it always seems there are more regulations and limitations than ever. In a free market, if someone is willing to pay what we charge, which is the market price, then we are not making too much profit.

"For example, the Time Guides projected profit is $434 billion. That is a lot of profit, and yes, we would be paying a lot of taxes. But I am guessing that many politicians will want to get their hands on that profit through taxes or find another way to get control over something this big. Irrespective of government pressure, I do like the idea of providing scholarship opportunities for those who are financially unable to take advantage of Timeport. I also believe we should be strategic in using large amounts of that profit to make a difference in education and to provide food for the needy, to name two worthy causes."

Karena paused then said, "I forgot to answer the second question. Any profit is enough profit, but more is always better. But let's remember, profit is only one of our criteria."

I chimed in. "I have one more question. What would be a showstopper for you on a business opportunity—something that would kill the opportunity no matter how good it is in terms of other criteria?"

Rory Williams answered first. "A moderate to high safety risk to our employees or to the people we bring to our time."

Shannon Block added, "A high risk of escape for customers we take to the past or ancestors we bring to the future."

Rashad Ford said, "Too much risk that our presence could change the space/time continuum—in other words, change the present because we disturbed the events of the past."

Kay then stood up and announced, "At this time, Mike and I will leave you in the capable hands of the executive team while we determine who the winner of the Teamwork Sharks challenge will be. Since Mike and I rarely agree, we will be back either after we are too bloodied to argue anymore, or until he gives up and lets me pick the winner!" She paused to let the audience enjoy a hearty round of laughter. "The execs will remain here to answer any questions you have about Timeport."

CHAPTER 36

Time for the Sharks to Circle

———

As usual, Kay did not waste any time. "Let's evaluate each one quickly versus the criteria, and see how much we agree or disagree. I will start with Time Guides. I believe it has little potential for disturbing the course of history because the purpose is to observe a historical event, not be in the center of the event. UST can take measures to avoid leaving any environmental time garbage. The profit is the greatest of all the finalists, but there is not much of a positive impact on society."

I mostly agreed. "Great analysis, Kay. Ray has always had me convinced that these profit numbers are very achievable. I only disagree in one area. I do believe there is risk that the filming of the past event will cannibalize its own revenue. Once we have the film, there won't be as much demand among potential new customers to return to the past, and that is what makes this business opportunity most profitable."

I then continued with my assessment of Making Cryogenics Obsolete. "I don't really like this one. Its risk of altering history is low, and it actually is a safer alternative than cryogenics where deaths do happen due to malfunctioning of the equipment. My main concern is that even though there is potential to capture a $28 billion market, the Timeport reservation purchase is for ten, twenty, or fifty years into the future. A lot can happen during that time to put the financial commitment at risk. I say we pass on this one."

Kay looked at me in disbelief. "I'm stunned! That's two in a row where we mostly agree. This is going to ruin our reputation."

I laughed and said, "Okay, let's talk about Generational Family Reunions. I have to give Sarah a lot of credit. She was very genuine, and she appealed to the audience with objectivity and logic as well as emotion and the betterment of society. There are few safety issues and little risk of disturbing the past. The gross revenue is similar to that of the Time Guides, and she has a plan for how to give back to society with the scholarship reunions for those who can't afford the fees."

"Sarah did a great job," Kay replied. "There was something that bothered me, though, and I almost hate to say it. It almost seemed that she was proposing this business opportunity for her own personal reasons. She so desperately wants to see her mother and brother again. I want to kick myself for saying it, but it did come across that way to me."

"I think Sarah's personal motivation is a strength," I countered, "but I am concerned about her lack of leadership experience for such a business opportunity with such great potential.

Kay was ready to tackle the next one. "Let's shelve that one for now, and go on to Space Travel Acceleration. I was very impressed with Benjamin, and how he rose above his fears. Although this is not as profitable as some of the others are, and it may not make as large an impact on society, it is probably the most achievable. Plus, it won't cause the tax man and regulators to come a-callin', and it is closely aligned with UST's core services. I am very in favor of this."

I laughed. "Finally we disagree, and I couldn't disagree more. This opportunity is different because, in essence, it would transport people into the future where the events are not already known. That causes a host of questions, risks, and concerns. Yes, it's aligned with UST's core services, but the profit does not move the needle much. This would be my last choice. Sometimes I think you gravitate to those who ask for help so your guidance can be associated with their success."

Kay stood up and walked a few paces to relieve her frustration. In a stern voice, she said, "How can you have such an opposite viewpoint when we heard the same presentations and heard the same criteria? You're acting like there is no risk to going into the past. I would put this at the top of my list precisely because the profit is not as much. I have a strong fear that the government is going to meddle in the business a lot more if the company is earning over $400 billion in profit in one year."

Feeling calmer now, she took her seat and added with a bit of a sarcastic smile, "And I forgive you for calling me biased when you know that's not true." Then with some humor, she said, "In the end, we will have a great debate on who should win—and then you will compromise."

After Kay and I discussed each of the business opportunities, we ranked our preferences from first to fourth, with first being most preferred and fourth being least preferred:

MIKE	
Family Reunions	1st
Time Guides	2nd
Making Cryogenics Obsolete	3rd
Space Travel Acceleration	4th

KAY	
Space Travel Acceleration	1st
Time Guides	2nd
Family Reunions	3rd
Making Cryogenics Obsolete	4th

When we saw that we only agreed on Time Guides as the second most preferred, Kay and I continued to make our case to each other using the criteria and the facts for each opportunity. There was some persuading and a lot of listening, and in the end, both of our rankings changed. It had been ninety minutes since we left the auditorium, but now we agreed on which business opportunity would win the Teamwork Sharks challenge.

I opened a box and took out the Teamwork Sharks Tooth Award that we had printed the previous day on the 3D Printer at UST. It was time to announce the winner.

Time for the Sharks to Circle

CHAPTER 37

And The Winner Is...

MANY OF THE AUDIENCE MEMBERS were standing outside the auditorium sipping coffee and enjoying some afternoon cookies set out on a table for them. When we were spotted, word spread quickly, and everyone finished their drinks and headed back to their seats. They didn't want to miss the announcement of the winner.

Karena was on stage waiting for us. It took a few minutes for the auditorium to fill up, and once it did, Karena made a few comments. "Let me just say how proud I am of the four of you who presented your case to Mike and Kay today. I knew they would be good, but your business plans were better than I expected and more creative, perhaps, than what we would have seen had the executives done this themselves. I am also proud of the other twenty-eight of you who submitted nominations as well as all of you in the audience who provided your input and engaged in this process. I am most thankful to Mike and Kay for their efforts as Teamwork Sharks. My father suggested we bring Mike and Kay here, and he was right. We are much farther along than we were four weeks ago when they arrived."

Karena turned to me and said, "And now, Mike will announce the winner."

It seemed that Sam and Marcus hadn't made it back. I had to admit I was a little disappointed at that. I wanted Sam to be there to share this moment with me, and to see how his brainchild acquisition of Timeport was about to take a big step in becoming commercialized.

Karena handed me the microphone when I reached center stage. I looked out at the eager faces and said, "Let me just say thank you again to all of you. I know I can speak for Kay. This has been the most enjoyable, challenging Teamwork Sharks experience we have ever had. All four of the business opportunities are very good. We had to consider the safety risk, the disturbance risk, protection against leaving any environmental time garbage, the impact on the customer's way of life, and the amount of profit involved. We also had to consider the impact of the opportunity on the core business of UST."

I paused because I could see the audience members whispering among themselves. Most likely they were making predictions as to who the winner would be. Chants of "Wong, Wong, Wong," rippled through the crowd, and "Sarah, Sarah, Sarah!" Others drowned them out with "Benjamin, Benjamin, Benjamin," and "Lina, Lina, Lina!" for Evangelina.

I looked at Kay, and she nodded that it was go time.

"Okay, everyone, we appreciate your enthusiasm!" I said, pausing to let them quiet down. "It is time to announce the winner. Let me tell you how honored we are to be part of this once-in-a-lifetime experience. As you know, we will definitely forget it." I smiled and waited.

There was a slight delay before everyone laughed, some of them taking a bit longer to get the joke.

"I wish we didn't have to forget this journey, but I've been told we'll go back to the good old days of 2016 not a bit wiser. Maybe we'll have some moments of déjà vu as the years pass and technology advances. One can dream! Anyway, back to the business at hand. Kay and I debated which business opportunity would be the best, biggest, and most profitable for UST. As usual, we disagreed and argued. But as you can see, there are no bruises, at least that are visible.

"Seriously, now, there can only be one winner, but all of these business opportunities have merit or they would not have made it to the final round. The winner definitely had a transformative idea and one that we believe is a gift to society, the world, and the solar system."

The crowd started again with chants of "Benjamin, Benjamin, Benjamin!"

I continued. "The winner has a personal mission about this business opportunity and will do anything to make it successful."

The chants shifted to "Sarah, Sarah, Sarah!" I wasn't finished.

"Yes, she had a very heartwarming story about how much this would mean to her, but she also convinced us that her idea would generate a lot of profit for a long time." The secret was out.

And The Winner Is...

"Sarah," I continued, lifting my voice over the cheers, "Kay and I believe your dream will come true. One day soon, you will reunite with your mother and brother. The dreams of many others will come true because we think you will be successful at leading this business opportunity. We believe you have what it takes to persuade people to help you make it a success. We believe Generational Family Reunions will be the first of many business opportunities that will make Timeport the recognized leader in time travel long before any competitors can get into the field. Congratulations, Sarah Serromaya!"

The audience clapped, whistled, and cheered, and someone started a fresh chant of "Sarah, Sarah, Sarah!"

"Come on up to claim your prize, Sarah!" Kay said, joining me at center stage.

As Sarah made her way to the front, hugging and high-fiving the whole way down the aisle, something caught my eye at the back of the room. I was thrilled to see Sam standing there clapping, a big smile on his face. He must have felt quite a sense of pride at that moment, of what he built. It was my sincerest hope that he was proud of his dad too.

Sarah came up to the stage, her face flushed with happiness. Kay held the Teamwork Sharks Tooth Award while I announced, "Sarah, I am so proud of you. You clearly have the characteristics of an innovative leader. I wish I could take you back to 2016 with us. I have several clients who could use someone like you on their leadership team. Congratulations, Sarah! You are the winner of the

Teamwork Sharks Tooth Award for UST in 2085." Kay and I each gave Sarah a big hug.

Sarah took the microphone to say a few words. "I want to thank Mike and Kay for this award. When I submitted the nomination, I did so out of a heartfelt desire to see a dream realized and to support the goals of UST because you wonderful people are my second family.

"We love you, Sarah!" somebody yelled.

"I love you more!" she replied. "But really, I wasn't motivated just to win this award. I have a strong desire to see my brother and mother again. But as I thought about that possibility, I felt very motivated to do the same for others. This will change our society for the better. I know, because I have watched it happen with the Goodfriends right here and now. Thank you, Karena, Marcus, and the entire leadership team."

With a tear in her eye, she looked up at the heavens as a way to acknowledge her mother and brother. She exhaled to collect her emotions and said, "Most of all, thank you, Sam, for making this happen with Timeport."

I wiped a tear and saw Sam do the same. I smiled at him across the crowd.

Sarah had one final statement. "I realize the leadership team now has to select any business opportunities they want to go forward with. So, to the leaders," she said, turning slightly to look at them, "please know that I may be young, but you can count on me and many others in this room to make Timeport a success that we can all be proud of. Thank you so much for this opportunity and this award." Turning back to the crowd, she said, "Let's do this!"

CHAPTER 38

Wrapping Things Up

Karena took the microphone as Kay and I took our seats at the side of the stage. "Wow!" she began, and the crowd responded with a fresh round of whoops and cheers. "What a day. I am proud of all of you. I am so proud of our winner, Sarah Serromaya. Sarah, I am so glad that you are on our team. You are more of an innovator and leader than I ever was at your age."

Karena started to choke up at what she had to say next. "The bad news is we have to say goodbye to Mike and Kay tomorrow after we meet to discuss the next steps in implementing Generational Family Reunions. Kay, Mike—you won't remember Marcus and me when you return to 2016, but we will always remember you."

Karena looked out at Sam. "Most of all, I know I can speak for Marcus and tell you, Dad, how proud we are of you—as an entrepreneur, an innovator, a father, grandfather, and a great grandfather. Thanks to you, we have this great company. None of it, including Timeport and all of the amazing possibilities it offers, would be here without you." The crowd spontaneously started chanting, "Sam, Sam, Sam." After what seemed like a long pause while Karena just stood and smiled at the crowd, she closed the event. "And now, I would like to say thank you, everyone. Enjoy your evening!"

I tried to take this moment in and enjoy it. I couldn't get my head around the fact that I was going back to my time the next day, and I wouldn't remember any of this. It would be as if I'd never met these great people. I actually entertained the idea of staying in 2085, but I missed Pam and I knew that I belonged in my time.

Marcus came up to me and gave me a big hug, "I am so glad I know my grandfather now. It means a lot to me. And the fun isn't over yet. Tonight we are having a going-away party for you and Kay at my house at seven. The whole family will be there."

CHAPTER 39

SOME TIME WITH GARY

GARY FLEW ME IN HIS skycar to the party, once again without Kay. She decided to spend her final evening with Roberto instead. They had become quite an item. Gary and I were pretty quiet in the car. Finally, I said, "Gary, do you think you will want your great great grandchildren to bring you back to their time to meet them?"

"I doubt it," said Gary. "I'm not some great man like you are."

I laughed at that remark. "Gary, I hope you can make it back to my time at some point. I am not a great man. I am lucky enough to have a great wife and son. I have a business that pays the bills, and I play baseball, my favorite sport, in my spare time—pretty ordinary life. My greatest accomplishment is here in the future based on what I see of my son and his entire family."

As we walked up to the door of Marcus's house, I told myself to enjoy this evening. I didn't want to think about the fact that by this time tomorrow, I wouldn't be here.

CHAPTER 40

A Party That I Will Definitely Forget

As we walked in the door, the party was already going. Karena came running up to me and gave me a big hug. "I can't believe you're going home tomorrow. I hope you have a great time with your family tonight."

I could tell everyone was having fun. The little kids were running around playing. We walked into the kitchen where all the adults were talking. When they saw me, they came over to give me a hug—Sam, Karena, Gary, Marcus, Debra, and my adult great grandchildren.

During an awkward moment of silence after a group hug, Marcus said, "Uh ... Mike, I am really sorry I missed the Teamwork Sharks event today. I guess that was pretty rude of me. Sam and I had to run an errand."

I wanted to reassure Marcus that it was a minor disappointment; besides, he and Sam had made it to the most important part of the meeting when we announced the

A Party That I Will Definitely Forget

winner. I just wanted to enjoy my last evening with my family. I decided to respond with some sarcasm to put him at ease. I'd discovered by now that Marcus had a great sense of humor.

"Well, Marcus, you're a lucky man that you get to escape my wrath. The good news is that by tomorrow, this will all be forgotten!"

Marcus had a bit of sly grin, as if I had just walked into his trap. "I don't think you're going to be angry if you turn around."

I turned and saw all the great, great grandchildren running to their parents all at once, grinning as if they were hiding a big secret. When the crowd parted, there was Pam. I rushed over to her and hugged her, and everyone started cheering.

Marcus said, "Dad and I didn't lie. We were running an errand—to go to 2016 to get Grandma and bring her back here for your going-away party. You should've seen what we went through explaining ourselves to her, not to mention prepping her for going through the Timeport tunnel! She finally said, 'Oh well, you only live once!' and she went through it like a pro."

Pam just grinned and said, "Here I am." We hugged again, and stood arm-in-arm gazing at our wonderful extended family.

Our time at the party zoomed by. Pam had so many questions. They told her that she wouldn't remember any of this tomorrow. It didn't matter to her. She was curious, just like I had been, and relished hearing all the details of everyone's lives.

It was a reminder to me that life is really about enjoying the moment whenever or wherever it is, not about what happened in the past or what will happen in the future.

CHAPTER 41

NEXT STEPS

PAM AND I ARRIVED AT UST bright and early so she could get a tour of the beautiful, future-modern office complex. She seemed so proud of Sam and her grandchildren for what they had created. Karena and Marcus were so happy that Pam could see this.

Kay entered the room and was totally surprised to see Pam. Taken aback, she exclaimed, "When did you get here? Roberto and I just came back from a quick trip around the world in space." She and Pam hugged each other in greeting. Pam had a twinkle in her eyes, and looked as if she was dying to ask about Roberto, who looked a little embarrassed but had a smile on his face that meant all was well with him and Kay.

Sam came into the room and said, "C'mon, Mom. Let's go get some coffee while these bigwigs talk business." Pam and Sam left the room.

Karena started the meeting with the leadership team and Sarah Serromaya. "As you all know, this is our last day with Mike and Kay, the Teamwork Sharks. I have talked to each of you individually, and we unanimously agree that Generational Family Reunions should go forward, and Sarah Serromaya should lead it. Mike and Kay, we would like your thoughts on next steps and any expectations we should set about teamwork within the team that Sarah forms."

Kay offered her thoughts. "Sarah, you are a natural leader, and I love your passion for this business opportunity. Executives, I encourage you to have confidence in her and provide her the support she needs. This launch team needs to consider all the ramifications of implementing this idea, from identifying Family Reunion customers to the return of the visiting family members back to their time after the reunion. Take special care that Sarah forms a team of highly competent people that are passionate about this project but care more about the team goals and outcomes more than their individual contribution. The team's first priority is to identify the goals and outcomes of this line of business that can only be achieved if they work well as a team."

Rashad Ford, the VP of Sales, said, "There is much at stake here. If you were to coach Sarah in leading this effort, how would you help her?"

"Great question, Rashad," I responded. "Here is what I would suggest."

- ▶ Select team members because of their competency, their integrity, and their passion for the team's goal.

Winning teams are made up of individuals who know how to win, and who pool that knowledge so that the group is better as a result.
- ▶ Get everyone on the same page. Agree on deliverables, responsibilities, interdependencies, the decision-making process, and the timeline. Keep score by tracking the team metrics. You have to know if you're winning.
- ▶ Sarah, you are a natural leader. Rely on your instincts.
- ▶ Achieve some early wins and publicize those wins. Success can be infectious. Make winning a habit.

Karena said, "Those are excellent suggestions. Sarah, it sounds like you have some work to do to kick this off. Mike, something tells me that we are going to need your help again. Would it be okay to bring you back if we need you?"

I was all in for that. "Absolutely, Karena, I wouldn't even have to think about that decision. Consider it done. Kay, are you open to returning?"

Kay's response was not as definitive. "Uh … yes, Karena, that sounds great, but can you and I discuss something privately before I go?"

"Sure, Kay," Karena replied.

The rest of us took that as our cue. When we got up and clustered in the hallway to say our goodbyes, I saw out of the corner of my eye Karena talking to Kay and smiling. There was something strange about that smile.

CHAPTER 42

CHANGE IN PLANS

Kay, Karena, Marcus, and I walked down to the Eva Goodfriend Timeport Operations Center (TOC). Sam, Pam, and Gary were there when we arrived.

Karena quickly laid out the plan. "Marcus will take you back to 2016 right before we arrived. You will emerge from Timeport near the dumpster at your office building. When you see Marcus, you will not know who Marcus is. He will ensure all is well with you before he comes back through Timeport. After Marcus returns to 2085, I will take Pam back to when we got her—the same day we came to get you and Kay."

"Who is taking Kay back?" I wondered. Karena and Kay looked at each other. Kay said, "I want to stay here a little longer and spend some more time with Roberto. Karena has agreed. I will be back. I just don't know when."

Pam, never able to resist a good love story, said, "Kay, you go girl. Enjoy your time with Roberto." Pam and I gave Kay a hug. I said to Kay, "You did a great job as a Teamwork Shark, but then you always do. We'll see you soon."

Karena said, "It's time to get ready. We need to prepare Timeport for our destinations. Marcus will go first then Mike. Mike, you will receive a hypnotic amnesia treatment as you enter the Timeport tunnel. The same thing will happen with Pam."

I handed Karena and Marcus a binder full of notes. "I have been keeping a journal about this Teamwork Sharks experience along with some tools and guidance. I want to leave it with both of you for safekeeping. Maybe it will be helpful to you when you explore additional business opportunities for Timeport. And yes, it's all here on paper. It's like you're holding a piece of history."

We shared a laugh, and Marcus said, "I love that it's a physical representation of all that we've accomplished together."

"Thank you so much," added Karena, hugging it to her as if it were a precious treasure.

It was pretty weird for Pam and me to say goodbye to Sam, Marcus, Karena, Gary, and Kay. Things got a bit emotional.

I said to Sam, "Not many fathers can see their son when he's in his eighties, and be amazed at what he has become. I hope someday to be as successful a businessman as you are, and to be as great a father as you are. I was proud of you when you were a boy, I was proud of you when you went off to LSU, and now I am proud of you when you are thirty years older than me. I love you, son." I couldn't hold back the tears any longer.

Sam gave me a big hug. "I love you too, Dad. You can't imagine what it feels like for me to have seen you after missing you for so many years. More importantly, it means so much to me that you met my family and that you and Kay are now part of what will be the history of Timeport. And Dad, most fathers don't have a chance to see their legacy in action. Timeport and my great family wouldn't be here today if it wasn't for you … and Mom of course."

Pam said in a half-joking way, "Some things never change. Sixty-nine years later, and I still feel like chopped liver when it comes to the two of you."

Sam and I looked at each other and laughed—just as we did sixty-nine years ago.

Finally, it was time to go. I wasn't sure what it would be like to say goodbye to my future family, but it felt like saying goodbye forever, at least until we could meet again in the future. It was almost like when you are dreaming, and you realize in the dream that it is a dream. Part of me wanted to wake up and get back to the reality of life in 2016, and part of me didn't want to leave the dream of living in 2085.

Despite my uncertainties, it was time to go back. I was ready.

CHAPTER 43

JUST ANOTHER DAY

I MUST HAVE ZONED OUT and come outside to throw some trash from my car into the dumpster. Funny, I didn't remember walking over to the dumpster after parking my car in the building parking lot.

In a daze, I walked toward the entrance to my office building when I saw a man who somehow looked familiar to me, probably about my age. He stopped and said, "How are you doing? You look familiar. Aren't you a CPA? You were a speaker at the CPA conference on Making Teamwork Profitable, right?"

"No wonder you looked familiar," I replied, reaching out to shake his hand. "Nice to see you again. My name is Mike."

He introduced himself. "Good to see you again, Mike. My name is Marcus. Maybe we'll see you at the next CPA event."

Seemed like a friendly guy.

When I walked into my office, the phone rang, and I could see that it was Pam from the caller ID.

I answered, "Are you at the office?"

Pam sounded very excited. "Yes, I just met another new friend in the parking garage. She said she had her own transportation business, so I gave her your card in case she needed a consultant. Her name is Karena."

Before I could reply, my cell phone rang. "I better get this," I said to Pam.

"Hi, Mike. My name is Rachel. We've never met, but my mother Kay Breeden has told me about working with you. Something strange has happened. There was a note on my door this morning in my mother's handwriting. The note said … uh … let me just read it to you. 'I will be out of pocket on a big project that just came up. I won't be able to contact you for a little while. Tell your sister Elaine not to worry. Not sure how long I will be gone, but when I come back, I know it will seem like it was yesterday when I left. Please tell Mike Goodfriend about this, and tell him to feel free to find another Teamwork Shark while I am gone.'" Rachel paused. "Mike, I am sorry to tell you this. But you know my mother. She will reappear like nothing happened."

"Yes, I know your mother well," I said. "But it's unusual for her to just disappear like this. We'll have to trust that she knows what she's doing."

I said goodbye to Rachel. The timing of this was not opportune, but I had been thinking that it was time to start engaging some other Sharks. Maybe this was a good opportunity for that.

EPILOGUE – ALL IS RIGHT WITH THE WORLD

Sam was in right field. A bucket of balls was on the ground next to me, and I was hitting fly ball after fly ball to him. It felt great to do this. Back when he played high school baseball, I hit bucket after bucket to him until I couldn't swing the bat anymore.

Sam was home from LSU for a long weekend. It was already the second semester of his freshman year. Time really flies. We hadn't done this since his final season of baseball as a high school senior. It reminded me how much we enjoyed this time together.

My thoughts wandered as I hit the balls. What would Sam achieve after college? Would he get married and have kids? Would I be alive to see his wife and kids?

Then, for no explainable reason, a feeling of calm confidence came over me. It was like I knew that things would turn out well for Sam. It was just a matter of time.

APPENDIX

Teamwork Sharks Journal
By Mike Goodfriend
For Universal Space Travel
February and March 2085

I decided to keep this journal to capture my thoughts for this Teamwork Sharks assignment. I think I will leave this with Karena and the leadership team when I go back to 2016.

February 16, 2085 – Cross-Functional Business Goals and TEAM IDENTITY

Cross-functional business goals can only be achieved when various functions and units within a company collaborate effectively as a team. UST's cross-functional business goal for their core business is to increase customer wallet share—to provide more core services to the same customer. TEAM IDENTITY is a core characteristic of the TeamScene® Model.

TEAM IDENTITY is about the team members seeing themselves as a single unit achieving a common or cross-functional goal. It is a good idea to assess how strong your TEAM IDENTITY is before you embark on a cross-functional initiative like increasing wallet share. Here are some of the TeamScene Teamwork Assessment items related to TEAM IDENTITY:

- Team members strongly believe in the team's vision—a strategic, breakthrough team goal to be achieved in three years or more.
- Team members willingly sacrifice their individual priorities to achieve the team's goals.
- Organizational silos are not negatively impacting how the team works together.
- Team members have the best interests of the team in mind.
- The team's leader holds team members collectively accountable for delivering on the team's objectives.
- Team members recognize one another for their contribution to the team's results.

February 17, 2085 – Delivering on Cross-Functional Goals: Start with a DEBATE

Before a team can UNITE with a Game Plan around its timeline for key deliverables for increasing customer wallet share, Roberto Rodriguez should bring together key UST

Appendix

leaders to debate the primary issues that will drive the Game Plan. Here are some of my recommendations to get the debate started:

- **Cross-functional metrics** – UST should define the metrics for measuring the increase in customer wallet share. I recommend tracking the increase in core services revenue by customer; specifically, revenue from multi-services vs. total revenue from that customer.
- **End-to-End Process Improvement** – UST's core services have always been delivered in an autonomous manner, focusing on process excellence within that core service. I recommend that UST consider an end-to-end coordinator role for each key customer. This coordinator will integrate the service experience from the mission plan to the outbound flight and the return spaceflight.
- **Reorganizing the Team Structure** – Most organizations have a primary organizational structure that supports how business gets done. This is what shows up on the organization chart, how roles are defined and how performance is assessed. For UST, the structure has been organized around the lines of business, such as Mission Planning and Astronaut Services, for example. I do not recommend a change in that structure, but I do recommend a "shadow structure" of cross-functional customer teams with a representative

from each core service who will focus on delivering an increase in wallet share for those customers.

▶ **Accountability for Each Key Customer's Wallet Share** – For each of the key customers, an appropriate leader needs to take ownership of delivering on the wallet share metrics. That leader needs to drive more integrated efforts between service lines to increase wallet share. I recommend that each executive, except Karena, be accountable for the increase in wallet share for three of each of the top twenty customers, and be the executive sponsor for each of the cross-functional customer teams in the shadow structure.

A "DEBATE of Opposing Views," as described in the TeamScene Model, is about learning collectively how Option A measures up against Option B or whether the pros of Option A outweigh the cons of Option A. A good debate is well planned and orchestrated so that those presenting their argument have time to prepare and gather facts. A good DEBATE of Opposing Views is not just between those presenting their arguments. The collective learning will be maximized if those hearing the DEBATE have an opportunity to add their perspective to the argument. The objective of a DEBATE in an organization about key issues is not to win. It is to learn collectively. Here are some of the items from the TeamScene Teamwork Assessment about DEBATE Opposing Views:

- The team allocates meeting time to discuss important business challenges.
- Team members solicit opposing views from one another.
- Team members listen to opposing views to understand the advantages and disadvantages of those views.
- Team members are effective at persuading one another.
- Team members appreciate unconventional thinking by other team members.
- Team member disagreements often lead to a breakthrough idea or solution.

February 28, 2085 – Innovation: Breakthrough or Disruptive?

Talking to some of the UST staff about various business opportunities they were considering for the Teamwork Sharks nomination made me consider what I had learned about innovation theory. Specifically, a theory called Disruptive Innovation became popular in the early 2000s. Clayton Christensen, the father of this theory, described disruptive innovations as opportunities at the low end of the market that turn non-consumers into consumers. These opportunities arise when companies focus on serving the high end of the market—the customers that will pay the most and expect the most from the product or service. This causes many potential customers at the low end of the market to not be served. They can't pay the higher prices, and they are less demanding about what they need from the product. This lack of service on the low end opens the door to disruptive innovations that can serve many more buyers with lower prices and fewer amenities.

Timeport is not really a disruptive innovation. It actually is a breakthrough innovation much like the computer technology industry. The computer started as a mainframe produced by IBM and sold at a very high price that only a few business customers could attain, as well as government. The desktop computer and then laptop computers were more disruptive than the mainframe, and new entrants into the market like Dell computers took market share away from IBM. But software skills were a limit to use and accessibility by many.

The smartphone was very disruptive to the computer market because its simplicity of use and the ability to do what a computer used to do could be accessed by many more consumers. Apple took market share from Dell and other computer manufacturers by developing innovative products that focused on the lower end of the market first then moved their way up the value chain with apps. These apps made it possible to do on a smartphone what previously could only be done on a laptop or desktop.

The Timeport technology is first to the market, and for many reasons, it makes sense to focus on the high end of the market—those customers who can pay the most and expect the most from it. But the lesson of the computer industry should teach UST that although they will probably have competitors in the beginning that focus on the high end of the market, there will eventually be disruptive innovation that focuses on the low end non-consumers making time travel available to many more. This will create an opening for those new competitors to move up the value chain over time and challenge what will likely be Timeport's dominant market share.

February 24, 2085 – Mining for Business Opportunities

The biggest challenge for a gold mining company is to determine where the gold is and thus where to dig the mine. Back in the Gold Rush days of the 1800s, once the area/region was known, miners came from everywhere to hopefully be the first to find that gold. They did this by using better techniques and working harder, and of course a fair amount of luck was involved.

Timeport is like a gold mine. The more miners are involved in that gold mine, the more gold will likely be discovered. Nominations were received today from thirty-two miners. Only four of them were executives. In talking to some of the UST staff while they were mining for business opportunities, we learned that they were bouncing ideas off each other and learning from other miners about their prospecting techniques. The executives should be commended for spreading the word to the UST employees about discovering the gold in the Timeport mine.

UST discovered a few secrets to mining for business opportunities:

Secret #1 – Don't keep your goldmine a secret in your organization if you need a lot of miners to help you find the most gold in the shortest amount of time.

Secret #2 – Involve as many miners as possible to explore as much of the goldmine as you can in a short period of time.

Secret #3 – Encourage miners to talk to each other and to learn from each other during the mining process.

March 1, 2085 – Making a Compelling Business Case
After reviewing thirty-two nominations for business opportunities and selecting nine for interview, Kay and I found some great ones and some that weren't ready. Kay presented the characteristics for making a compelling business case:

- **Be clear about what the business opportunity is** – the need it will serve, the market it will play in, what it will offer, and the marketplace advantage for Timeport and UST by being the first to the market for time travel.

- **Why you are compelled to lead this** – Tell your story for this business opportunity including why it matters to you and why you want to lead it.
- **Speak to the key stakeholders** – Align your message to make this a win for your key stakeholders: The Teamwork Sharks, the executives, the customers, and the business units/functions at UST.
- **Why this can ONLY be achieved as a team** – Describe the cross-functionality of the team and the roles of the team members.
- **Estimate the ROI** – Estimate the projected investment, revenue, and cost models for the business opportunity.

Kay and I thought Ray Wong made a compelling business case for the Time Guides business opportunity:

- The market was sightseeing travel for the very wealthy, especially those interested in history. The market advantage for UST comes with the filming of the event and making it available for download by those not able to afford Time Guides tours. That first-to-market advantage would make it difficult for a new competitor to copy.
- Ray was a history major in school and learned that what most of us know about history is based on the lens we learn it through—the historians who write the history. Since historians are human, there will

always be some amount of bias. Because of that, he saw Time Guides as an opportunity for people to explore the actual historical event through time travel to that event and through the downloadable films produced during the visit to the event.
- ▶ Ray spoke to Kay and me during the nomination process. He gave examples in his nomination that Kay and I could relate to, using historical events that were before 2016 instead of those after 2016 that we would not be able to relate to.
- ▶ Ray outlined the planning and execution team for Time Guides, and the coordination and teamwork required for the team to execute this opportunity in a safe manner.
- ▶ Ray did a great job of outlining the revenue and profit model, both of which are exponentially greater than UST's core business.

Ray and eight other nominees were selected to be interviewed because they made compelling business cases, but I wanted to highlight Time Guides as a model for submitting proposed business opportunities.

March 5, 2085 – Successful Interviewing

Anyone who proposes a business opportunity that makes it to the second round of evaluation, such as interviews in the case of the Teamwork Sharks process, needs to realize how their role as proposer changes. They have to be able to do the following effectively:

- Effectively articulate the case verbally, not just in writing.
- Present only the facts and justifications that make the most impact.
- Make their passion for the business opportunity visible.
- Demonstrate how the business opportunity will satisfy the criteria that the executives set as requirements for the nominees.
- Be ready for the devil's advocate—someone who will challenge you with an opposing view.
- Consider the most significant risks to the business opportunity and a strategy for mitigating them.

March 12, 2085 – Being Successful on Stage

The finalists did a great job today with their presentations. Here are some thoughts from today and other finalist pitches to the Teamwork Sharks:

- **Get everyone's attention immediately** – Ray Wong asked the audience to share a historical event that shaped who we are today. Sarah Serromaya told the audience about wanting to see her brother again. He died after being hit by a car.

- **Make it conversational** – Too many presenters want to launch right in with the perfect set of slides and bullet points they want to communicate. Being too scripted can make people skeptical about your message. Two-way conversations help people trust each other. The same is true in a presentation. For example, when we challenged Sarah Serromaya about whether she might burn out, she responded by having a two-way conversation with us.
- **Keep props to a minimum** – Evangelina Walker had a body builder carrying a tub of ice. She put chicken meat in the ice to make a point about cryogenics. Although this was a great attention getter, it may have been too much distraction for some. It may have drawn too much attention to the prop, thus making it more difficult for the audience to focus on Evangelina and her message.
- **Be confident, passionate and lively** – We had a Teamwork Sharks finalist in 2014 who was sweating and wiping his forehead during the presentation. He ended up winning because his passion and confidence told us that he was nervous because he wanted his idea to be selected.
- **Appearance matters** – All the presenters today were dressed in appropriate professional attire. Always dress one step better than your audience. If the audience is in jeans and you're in a tuxedo, you put too much distance between you and the audience.

- **Be ready for the uppercut** – In a boxing match, the uppercut is often used as a knockout punch. In a process like the Teamwork Sharks where the audience and the Teamwork Sharks are looking to test whether the business opportunity is worthy of winning and/or being supported by the organization, questions and challenges will serve as a knockout punch. Ray Wong did an outstanding job with a great business opportunity, but the question about the cannibalization of the time travel event by having the video available for download was an uppercut. It made him more vulnerable to another competing finalist with an equally strong business opportunity.
- **Close the deal** – In sales methodology, closing the deal requires an appeal to the decision maker, whether through emotion or fact, that sets you apart from the competition and creates a sense of urgency for a decision in your favor. Kay and I believed that Sarah was the best in terms of meeting all the criteria outlined by the executive team: exponentially high profits, positive impact on society without altering history and with minimal risk for environmental time garbage and safety issues. Time Guides was not far behind. After Kay and I had some debate and disagreement, we agreed that Sarah had the best, biggest, and most profitable business opportunity. She closed the deal for Generational Family Reunions through her passion and commitment.

Tomorrow will be our final meeting with the executives and Sarah Serromaya to discuss next steps for forming the Generational Family Reunions team. Timeport is a breakthrough innovation. The Generational Family Reunions team can achieve some great things.

This opportunity reminds me of a special baseball team I played for back in about 2007. The team was called the Heartbreakers. Our manager, Dave Deal, picked the name. It was not a typical team name like the Astros, the Cardinals, or the Yankees. We were the only team in the whole league without uniforms or hats with a team name or logo on them. We wore plain black shirts and plain black hats. Dave wanted us to be underestimated. Dave wanted to "break some hearts"—in baseball that is.

Several of the opposing teams underestimated us during the regular season. We were no longer being underestimated when we won our way to the championship game against the Rangers, who were perennial champs. Unfortunately, the timing was not good for us. The day of the championship, only seven of our players showed up. As most of you know, you need nine players to field a full baseball team. In our league, you are allowed to play with seven players. You can borrow two fielders from the other team, but they don't bat for you. When their spots in the batting order come up (eighth and ninth), you take automatic outs, but not if the automatic out would be the third out of an inning.

Dave had his own game plan, and we all got behind it. He proposed that we not borrow two fielders and instead play

Appendix

with only our seven in the field. Of course, most would say that is a crazy strategy to build a game plan around, especially in 95-degree June heat without a second baseman and an outfielder on a field almost the size of a major league field. But the advantage was that we wouldn't have to take any outs while we batted. When Dave presented his rationale to us, he made the following points:

- ▶ He preferred our seven players in the field to having two of their players who probably wouldn't play their best.
- ▶ He liked what our seven players could do to produce runs, and he didn't want the disadvantage of having to take an automatic one or two outs when we were batting.
- ▶ He believed it would be a lot more fun because we would all probably bat five or six times.
- ▶ He thought this might make the opposing team overconfident in their assumption that a team with only seven players could never win a championship game.

It didn't take him long to convince us. We knew we had nothing to lose and everything to gain. We quickly developed our game plan. Dave prepared the batting order, and the rest of us made our fielding adjustments. I was our team's right fielder, but that day, I shared the entire outfield with another player. He was the left center fielder, and I was the right center fielder. The infielders also had to make adjustments because the shortstop and first baseman had to determine when each of them would need to cover second base and when second base would not be covered. What Dave didn't say was something we all knew. Dave was probably the best pitcher in the league even with very bad knees. Dave would keep us in the game. We just needed to back him up by making great plays in the field.

I learned a lot about how a team could Unite with a Game Plan:

- ▶ The best strategy is one that exploits your advantages, even if you are disadvantaged.
- ▶ A team's leader can make the best decisions for a game plan, autocratically. But to unite the team, s/he has to engage the team to get feedback by having a debate or by persuading the team of his/her rationale.
- ▶ You need to have the right players to execute your strategy. They need to be talented, skilled, optimistic, and team-oriented.
- ▶ When you don't have the resources you need, set priorities to maximize what you can accomplish as a team.
- ▶ You have to adjust your roles and responsibilities to fit the strategy.
- ▶ The right game plan inspires confidence in the team members and stretches them to perform at higher levels.

Did we win the game? Did we deliver the championship? The game was very close right up to the end. Clearly, the

Rangers were frustrated that they couldn't dominate us. Our team's positive attitude and belief that we could win fueled us to play above expectations. We played with aggressiveness and hustle in the field. We all batted at least six times and put nine runs on the board. It was tied going into the latter stages of the game when the Rangers put runners on second and third, and an unlikely hero hit a ground ball directly to where the second baseman would have been (if we'd had one) to score two runs that were the game winners.

Although we lost the game, I was only mildly disappointed. The outcome probably would not have been any better if we had borrowed their fielders. If you saw us walking off the field that day and didn't know the score, you would have thought we won, and if you saw the looks on the faces of the Rangers walking off the field, you would have thought they lost that game. Clearly, we united as a team behind Dave's game plan. The Rangers had a clear advantage that day, but they did not unite as a team like we did. We had just as much opportunity to win that game as the Rangers did, and that felt like a victory. Yes, a victory would have been sweet. We were so close to being the ultimate heartbreakers.

We became an exceptional team that day. Teamwork didn't get us a win on the scoreboard, but it did the following season when that teamwork helped us win the championship. There was never a doubt. If we could almost beat the perennial champs using only seven players, we knew nothing would stop us the next time around.

I want the Generational Family Reunions team to experience the joy of being on a great team. The game of business is different from the game of baseball, but from what I have seen, great teams in business can experience the same joy of working together to accomplish a goal and to meet a challenge that no one thought was possible. Examples of this include doubling the company's profit through an improvement in on-time delivery from 70 percent to 95 percent in one year, working as a cross-functional team to launch an innovative service to the existing market, and aligning different functions on a major project to achieve exceptional project results.

When I go back to 2016, I hope that I will remember everything about 2085 including Timeport and all of you at UST, especially Sam, Marcus, Karena, and the rest of my family. I love you all. Thanks for the experience of a lifetime!

ACKNOWLEDGEMENTS

I believe we all have a book in us. I would like to acknowledge the special people who were there for me during this project:

Lance Mosby – I would like to thank you for reading the first draft of my manuscript. I knew I could count on you for your honesty, advice and encouragement. As the project progressed, you continued to provide ideas and thought-provoking suggestions every step of the way. I am proud to call you my friend.

Carrie Saks – I also want to express my thanks to you for reading my first draft. The documentation of your "play-by-play" observations gave me a clear picture of what the reader might be thinking. It was great having the perspective of someone who knew Sam since he was a young child.

Kay Breeden – Without you, the Teamwork Sharks would just have been another idea of mine that never came to fruition. I will never be able to thank you enough for sharing your expertise and for collaborating with me to launch the Teamwork Sharks concept. I have been fortunate to receive the gift of your belief in me.

Clients and Colleagues – Thank you for being my teacher for more than 25 years. It is through the integration of those experiences with all of you that gave birth to the Teamwork Sharks.

Family and Friends – I could think of no better way to honor all of you than by making the names and attributes of the characters in this book a reflection of you.

Pam – I am lucky to be married to you and have you as my partner in life. Your enduring patience, understanding and love helped me achieve something I never I thought I could do – be an author.

Sam – We are so proud and blessed to have you as our son. You provided me the inspiration to write this book. Without you, there would be no *Breakthrough Time*.

Acknowledgements

Unleashing the Value of Unrealized Business Opportunities

Visit teamworksharks.com

The Teamwork Sharks Leadership Challenge:
Invest in Your Next Generation of Leaders

The Teamwork Sharks Strategy Challenge:
Realize Your Unique Market Advantage

The Teamwork Sharks First Step: Are the Teamwork Sharks What Your Organization Needs?

Book Mike Goodfriend as Your Speaker:
- Leadership Development Breakthroughs
- Mining for Business Opportunities
- Supercharge Your Strategic Planning

Visit goodfriendconsulting.com

TeamScene®: The Teamwork Competency Model for Leadership Teams

Making Teamwork and Leadership Profitable:
- Teamwork Engineering
- Leadership Coaching
- Meeting Facilitation

Mike Goodfriend
mike.goodfriend@teamworksharks.com
(713) 789-6840

ABOUT THE AUTHOR

Michael Goodfriend created the Teamwork Sharks to guide companies on the best practices for implementing new ideas and ventures through teamwork. Many companies use the Teamwork Sharks to invest in their next generation of leaders or supercharge their strategic planning.

Michael also developed TeamScene®, a teamwork competency model for leadership teams, to help improve teamwork dynamics in the business world. When he consults with leadership teams, he uses experiential project-planning exercises, develops the innovator's mind-set, rebuilds trust in team members' working relationships, develops core values, and aligns roles and responsibilities. Michael is also a Breakthrough Leadership Coach.

When he first started out, Michael worked for Price Waterhouse Coopers as a CPA. He was a board member for the Houston CPA Society and Big Brothers Big Sisters of Greater Houston. Michael earned the senior certification in the Birkman Method personality profile. He also led a group of certified Birkman consultants for six years.

When he's not leading a Teamwork Sharks session or writing, he likes to watch or play baseball.

www.ingramcontent.com/pod-product-compliance
Lightning Source LLC
Chambersburg PA
CBHW070238190526
45169CB00001B/221